WHAT COLOR IS YOUR PARACHUTE?

GUIDE TO ———————

RETHINKING

RESUMES

Write a Winning Resume and Cover Letter
and Land Your Dream Interview

RICHARD N. BOLLES

TEN SPEED PRESS
Berkeley

Published in the United States by Ten Speed Press, an imprint of the Crown Publishing Group, a division of Random House LLC, a Penguin Random House Company, New York.
www.crownpublishing.com
www.tenspeed.com

Ten Speed Press and the Ten Speed Press colophon are registered trademarks of Random House LLC.

Library of Congress Cataloging-in-Publication Data

Bolles, Richard Nelson.
    What color is your parachute? guide to rethinking resumes : write a winning resume and cover letter and land your dream job / by Richard N. Bolles.
        pages cm
    Includes index.
    1. Résumés (Employment) 2. Cover letters. 3. Job hunting. I. Title.

    HF5383.B553 2014

    650.14'2--dc23

                                2014005257

Trade Paperback ISBN: 978-1-60774-657-7
eBook ISBN: 978-1-60774-658-4

Printed in the United States of America

Design by Margaux Keres

10 9 8 7 6 5 4 3 2 1

First Edition

CONTENTS

1 PREPARING TO WRITE YOUR RESUME

RETHINKING WHAT A RESUME IS

Yeah, I think I know what you want. You want me to get right to it. Tell you how to write a winning resume, give you an outline or template, tell you how to fill it in, tell you where to post it. And that's that.

Well, much as I would love to do that, I just can't.

Resumes need a lot more thought these days. Since the Great Recession of 2008, resumes aren't working too well.

I'm guessing you knew that.

Everyone assumes this is because there are no jobs these days.

Well, there are jobs. I'm looking at the government's little-known report, sitting here on my desk right now. It's called JOLTS for short, but its full name is *Job Openings and Labor Turnover Survey*. You can look it up on the Internet. It's issued monthly. This one is for January 2014. It reports that during that month, 4,500,000 people in the United States found jobs, and there were still 4,000,000 vacancies unfilled at the end of that month. That's a total of 8,500,000 vacancies filled or waiting to be filled. That month! That's pretty typical in the United States. Every month.

Now admittedly, that's not enough jobs or enough vacancies to fix our distressing unemployment problem. Still, *somebody's* getting those eight million jobs. Each month.

Why shouldn't you be among them?

Well, one reason—a *big* reason—may be your resume.

It almost certainly needs fixin'.

Yesterday's resumes just aren't up to the task today.

Yesterday's resumes are like a dull knife trying to cut food. Need sharpening. Badly.

These days, you can't just fill out a resume, post it, and expect it to go anywhere.

Resumes now take more time than they used to.

They take more thought than they used to.

In this economic climate, you have to work harder to make yours effective, in finding those jobs that are out there.

But you can do it. Yes, you can.

That's what this little book is about.

Let's start simple, with some thinking. Or, rethinking.

LET'S START SIMPLE

Okay, here's the story:

You want to find work. To find it, you've got to secure an interview with some employer or employers who actually have the power to hire you. And employers are busy people. They're not necessarily anxious to spend all day doing interviews. So, since you know that, you send someone on ahead of you, to plead your case for you.

And that *someone* is not actually a person but a piece of paper.

Yes, you send a piece of paper on ahead of you, to make the case as to why you should be invited in for an interview. And that piece of paper has a name. It is called a *resume*. Or resumé. Or résumé. Or its near cousin, CV (*curriculum vitae*, meaning "the course of my life").

Now, the most interesting thing about this piece of paper (digital or real) is that while it looks like just a bunch of words, it really is a painting. And that's because employers have the same thing you do: *imagination*.

Yes, your resume looks like just words. A lot of words. But when they're reading your resume, the words are lifting off the page and painting a picture of you in the imagination of the employer who reads it.

Employers wouldn't call it a painting; they would call it an "impression" of you. Same thing. They are looking at this piece of paper, covered with words, but they are thinking in terms of pictures. They are visualizing you.

Now, here's the question. Do the words they read make them visualize you as a competent worker, or not? Do the words they read make them visualize you as energetic, or not? As joyful, or not? As a team player, or not? As honest, or not?

And let's throw in: Do they visualize you as *tall, short,* or *average height? Young, middle-aged,* or *old?* Yes, those things aren't covered in your resume, but employers can't turn their imaginations off, just because they've finished looking at this piece of paper you sent on ahead of you. Rightly or wrongly, they see, they imagine, beyond your words. That's just human nature.

But to my main point: It's not just words that determine whether or not they decide to call you in for an interview. It's the picture of you that these words paint in an employer's imagination that determines whether they invite you in, or not.

So, when you set out to compose your resume, you would do well to think of yourself overall as a painter, not a writer. Your paintbrushes are your words. What is the *picture* of you that they paint? That is the question you should ask yourself, when you—or someone you hire—are debating what words to set down in your resume.

EIGHT SECONDS

Let's say you see a job posting. Some employer is looking for someone to fill a vacancy or a job newly created. You send in your resume. And you want to know how long an employer will likely spend looking at this resume/painting of you that you are sending on ahead, to plead your case for you. The answer will vary, of course.

There's a difference, for example, between how long the owner of a restaurant will spend looking at the resume you drop off, when you are applying to become the manager there, versus how long a multibillion-dollar corporation will spend looking at your resume when 250 came in that day. With a small employer you might get as much as two minutes. With larger employers, we know (*because people have measured it*) that generally your resume will get between four and fifteen seconds of attention. The average is eight.

Eight seconds! Yikes! An employer is going to be reading down your resume fast. In fact, they may not get all the way to the bottom in those eight seconds. So, what they read first, what they see in the top half or even top third of your resume, is going to be determinative.

What can you do about *that*?

What can you do about this painting that the employers may be taking only a fast look at?

Well, real painters of course paint in various ways. But, as we can tell from the sketchbooks of famous painters like Rembrandt (right*), they usually begin by laying down in broad strokes the outline of the whole portrait or picture. Then later they fill in. Details, shading, and such.

If your resume is only going to get eight seconds of attention, then it must do something like that. In the top third of your resume you must lay down in broad strokes an outline of who you are, using the words you write. Enough to make the employer hungry to see what else you have to say for yourself, as during the remaining two-thirds you shade and fill in. So to speak.

KEY WORDS OR *KEYWORDS*

The new wrinkle of our day and age, regarding resumes, is key words. In the old days—ten or twenty years ago, say— you never heard about these. But now, article after article on the Internet will emphasize the importance of your putting *key words* near the top of your resume. Everyone thinks it's because of computers and scanning software. And that's a great part of it, sure.

---

*A Sheet of Studies (1630s), by Rembrandt Harmensz van Rijn.

But not solely. Eventually the eyes of a real human are going to be looking at your resume. Key *words,* like all the other words on your resume, are paintbrushes. But it is the peculiar task of *key words* to lay down, in bold strokes, near the very top of your *painting*—excuse me, resume—the broad outline of who you are, which the rest of your resume is then going to fill in. If the employer's eyes get down that far.

Now, this term is normally spelled *keywords.* But the dictionary permits the term to be spelled as two separate words, and throughout this guide I spell it as two separate words.

Why? Because in my working with job-hunters I have discovered that altogether too many of them think *keywords* are a separate animal, with an official list from which you choose, and that sort of thing. No, they are just words—any words—that are key to understanding the job under discussion, and what you have to offer. Most any word, noun or verb, may become key to understanding a job . . . or You.

And you want those key words near the top of your resume.

Here's one example, starting on next page.*

---

*Yes, it's a two-page resume. This will strike terror into the hearts of those who feel a resume must *never* be more than one page. But so many are. So many *successful* ones are. (Another "rule" out the window.)

Name
Contact information

SENIOR MARKETING MANAGER

Product Marketing	Channel Marketing	Marketing Communications	Corporate Marketing

Accomplished, results-driven marketing leader with a strong background in marketing communications, channel partnership programs, branding, and product launches in major high-tech companies. Proven track record of turning around struggling products and driving significant sales revenue and growth. Manage multimillion-dollar budgets and collaborate with executives to design integrated marketing strategies. Key qualifiers include:

- Marketing / Communications
- Advertising
- Direct Marketing
- Lead Generation
- Collateral Production

- Branding
- Messaging
- Positioning
- Partnership Engagement
- Social Media

- Sales Strategies
- Channel Marketing
- B2B / B2C Launches
- Communication Plans
- SEO / SEM

- Online Marketing
- Database Segmentation
- Website Development
- Forecasting
- Email Marketing

PROFESSIONAL EXPERIENCE

SYMMETRY MARKETING AND DESIGN, Foster City, CA   2004–present
Marketing Consultant

Provided marketing, business development, branding, design, messaging, and sales development expertise to a variety of start-up businesses. Branding, marketing and corporate strategy coaching.

VERIFONE, INC., San Jose, CA
Global Marketing Manager

Developed marketing and product planning strategies and provided expertise on digital marketing, product information, and marketing integration during acquisitions. Led two major product releases and directed creative agencies. Ensured alignment between marketing strategies and corporate initiatives.

- Successfully integrated marketing collateral for global products during two multibillion-dollar acquisitions.
- Launched two flagship product lines to grow and capture POS market share, achieving the #1 position in the U.S.
- Initiated security campaigns that drove the awareness of company leadership in the payment security landscape.
- Supported innovative security product offerings and mobile retailing solutions, reducing costs and turnaround time.
- Extended into new media markets, developing strong channel partnerships with Google, PayPal, and others.
- Supported field sales, closing business with major clients, including Target, Microsoft, Trader Joe's, and Chase Bank.

SONY ELECTRONICS, INC., San Jose, CA
Product Marketing Manager, 2006–2010

Successfully turned around and grew a mature product line through solution marketing, channel partnerships, and sales incentives. Developed and maintained strategic partnerships and channel marketing programs. Led outbound marketing, communications, and business development. Maintained full P&L responsibility. Trained, managed, and coached a team of high-performing sales consultants. Managed advertising agencies, researched competitive positions, and implemented key account engagement programs. Maintained consistent brand image and positioning.

- Renegotiated Symantec relationship and launched new multilevel bundled software offering, growing sales.
- Retrained and turned around underperforming sales / marketing team, increasing performance 50% in one year.
- Developed annual marketing plans, resulting in incremental annual sales of $3M, a 30% sales increase.
- Managed 40-model product line representing $65M in solution sales and $70M in components sales revenue.
- Communicated with 5 distribution partners and 500 VARs, including HP, Symantec, MiraPoint, Intradyn, and GE.

SONY ELECTRONICS, INC., San Jose, CA (Continued)
Solution Marketing Manager, 2005–2006

Created successful go-to-market strategies for new solutions and developed global Marcom and business development initiatives. Built a high-performing team of marketing and sales professionals. Managed external vendor relationships and developed sales channels with distribution, reseller, and VAR partners.

- Grew annual sales from $1.8M to $11M, exceeding product goals and annual targets.
- Achieved 197% sales growth through an integrated approach to sales, awareness, and brand identity.
- Delivered groundbreaking go-to-market strategy that propelled the business unit into a position of global leadership.
- Updated channel sales program, leading to new strategic partnerships and increased sales.

Marketing Manager - Consultant, 2004–2005

Successfully launched new corporate business unit and established long-term strategic partner relationships, generating incremental YoY growth. Implemented marketing communications initiatives. Collaborated with global marketing teams to orchestrate product launches. Planned events and ensured alignment between sales and business strategies. Trained internal and external sales teams. Collaborated with engineers to create technical marketing materials and white papers.

- Developed a Dealer Certification and incremental sales programs and defined key business strategies.
- Improved the lead-qualification process, accelerating the sales cycle while achieving a record closing rate.
- Managed creative agencies, vendors, and ad agencies producing marketing materials and programs.

Marketing Communication Consultant, 2001–2004

Established an in-house advertising and Marcom department and supported multiple consumer and business solution product lines. Created high-quality advertising, lead generation, collateral, direct marketing, and email marketing programs. Managed project budgets and maintained optimal ROI. Scheduled and negotiated contracts with vendors.

- Managed the production of various digital materials, including websites, emails, banners, and e-newsletters.
- Created and analyzed a high-volume direct mail program for product launches and promotions.
- Designed consistent channel incentive programs and end-user promotions.

EVOICE-AOL, Menlo Park, CA   2000–2001
Marketing Manager

Successfully grew a user base and managed a $10M budget. Implemented corporate marketing programs to generate brand awareness. Designed and analyzed advertising, direct marketing, web communications, and other collateral.

- Grew the user base from 200,000 to one million+ subscribers, reducing the cost of acquisition to an all-time low.

HITACHI SEMICONDUCTOR (AMERICA), INC., San Jose, CA   1998–2000
Marketing Communication Specialist - Contractor

Managed all marketing and communication activities and oversaw database migration. Oversaw corporate website.

- Integrated a new literature fulfillment process and improved web flow and lead generation.

AMERITECH, San Bruno, CA   1997–1998
Direct Marketing Specialist

Supported promotions, trade shows, and marketing collateral. Completed internal audits and direct marketing initiatives.

EDUCATION, TRAINING, AND COMPUTER SKILLS

Bachelor of Science in Business Administration in Marketing, San Francisco State University, San Francisco, CA

Training at Stanford in Web Design HTML, Strategic Marketing, and Graphic Design at Stanislaus State University in SEO / SEM

Microsoft Office, including Word, Excel, Outlook, and PowerPoint; Adobe Acrobat, Photoshop, and Illustrator; HTML

ELIMINATE, ELIMINATE

Still, you're puzzled.

Why do you have to write this way?

Why is an employer only giving you eight seconds?

What's the hurry? Why so fast? Why so brief? I mean, you may have slaved over that resume, hours on end, and now it only gets an eight-second look? Come on! What kind of game are employers playing?

Well, it's simple. They're not playing a game of hiring. They're playing a game of elimination. At least at the beginning.

They're faced with a problem bigger than you. On average, corporations, for example, get 250 resumes for each vacancy that they post or advertise.* When an employer is faced with such a large stack of resumes, real or digital, they go through that stack with one main obsession: "How can I cut the stack down to size?"

There are just too many job-hunters. Too many knocking on their door. Most especially now. When we're still recovering from the Great Recession of 2008. Employers are looking for ways to get it down to last man standing. Or last woman standing. Your sending them your resume just makes it easier for them.

---

*"Why You Can't Get a Job . . . Recruiting Explained by the Numbers," *ERE*, May 20, 2013, www.ere.net/2013/05/20/why-you-can't-get-a-job-recruiting-explained-by-the-numbers. I am indebted to Dr. John Sullivan, whose article this is, for taking the time and trouble to gather so many of the studies (and statistics) I cite here.

Later, it will be *Who can I choose?* But for now, it's *Who can I eliminate?* Elimination is the name of the game.

They're reading down your resume—fast—looking for one thing: a reason—any reason—to eliminate your resume, so they can cut their stack down to a manageable size that they can call in, at the end, for an actual interview. Incidentally, we know how many they're trying to end up with: just five or six. The average number of interviews employers need to conduct to find a hire stays pretty constant, year in, year out. It's 5.4 job-hunters. (*No, I don't know how they only interview .4 of one of those people!*)

Eliminate, eliminate, eliminate, eliminate. Playing this game of elimination represents a time savings for the employer. As it only takes a typical employer about eight seconds to scan a resume with their eyes, they can get rid of fifty job-hunters—*I mean turn down fifty resumes*—in five minutes or less. Whereas, interviewing those fifty job-hunters in person would have required a minimum of twenty-five hours. *Great* time savings!

AN EMPLOYER'S SCANNING SOFTWARE

If it's a large organization, they can speed up the elimination game even more, by first putting your resume through automatic resume scanning software—technically called ATS (applicant tracking system) or ERM (electronic resume management) systems.[*]

---

[*]Janine Truitt, "When Applicant Tracking Systems Attack," *ERE,* July 26, 2012. www.ere.net/2012/07/26/when-applicant-tracking-systems-attack.

The more sophisticated—which is to say, the more expensive—of these ATSs can be set to look not just for key words, but also for other words that usually are near that key word when it is authentically used, and if the software doesn't find that—if you just tossed that key word in there because you thought it sounded good—they will screen you out.

At which point, as the scientist Kenan Sahin points out, this may technically still be software but it behaves more like a "robot" (though not as we typically think of robots). And this process doesn't take the software/robot eight seconds; it just takes a fraction of one second.

All this *may* happen, *if* it's a large organization. (These systems are expensive. They can cost thousands, on up into the millions. Therefore, small employers—250 or fewer employees—are not likely to have them.)

But jobs aren't all with large organizations: 66 percent of the jobs in this country are, in fact, with organizations that have just 1–250 employees; 18 percent are with organizations that have 251–1,000 employees; and only 16 percent are with still larger organizations. *

Okay then, how common are ATSs in large organizations? You will find the following answer all over the Internet: *If it's a large organization, they will for sure electronically scan*

---

*Reported by Regina Pontow, author of *Proven Resumes* (Ten Speed Press).

your resume, which means you run the risk of software rejecting you, not a human—if it doesn't find the proper key words, or your resume isn't formatted properly, or it uses the wrong font. All large organizations do this.

Well, maybe.

But there was a survey—done by BYU professors—that discovered 60 percent of the Fortune 500 companies surveyed did not electronically scan the resumes they received. They input the data manually, if they input it at all.[*] The wastebasket or shredder was and is always an alternative. So who knows? Maybe all large organizations do use an ATS; maybe all large organizations don't. Take your pick.

All you need to know is that these days there is *a chance* that your resume may get scanned by software before it gets scanned by human eyes. So, you *must* prepare for this possibility.

Mentally prepare, as well as taking practical steps in the formatting and such.

Best mental preparation? Remember, this is no big deal: just another step—an extra step—in the game employers are initially playing with your resume anyway—the game of *Elimination*.

Here's an infographic overview showing how all of this plays out in a typical large organization:

---

*Reported by John Feldmann in www.theundercoverrecruiter.com/ creative-resumes-how-much-too-much.

THE ELIMINATION GAME*

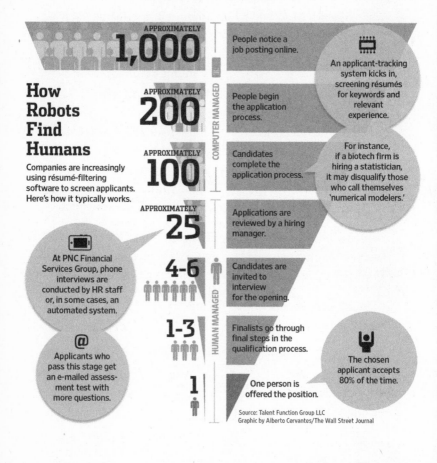

How Robots Find Humans

Companies are increasingly using résumé-filtering software to screen applicants. Here's how it typically works.

COMPUTER MANAGED

APPROXIMATELY **1,000** — People notice a job posting online.

An applicant-tracking system kicks in, screening résumés for keywords and relevant experience.

APPROXIMATELY **200** — People begin the application process.

For instance, if a biotech firm is hiring a statistician, it may disqualify those who call themselves 'numerical modelers.'

APPROXIMATELY **100** — Candidates complete the application process.

APPROXIMATELY **25** — Applications are reviewed by a hiring manager.

At PNC Financial Services Group, phone interviews are conducted by HR staff or, in some cases, an automated system.

HUMAN MANAGED

4-6 — Candidates are invited to interview for the opening.

Applicants who pass this stage get an e-mailed assessment test with more questions.

1-3 — Finalists go through final steps in the qualification process.

The chosen applicant accepts 80% of the time.

1 — One person is offered the position.

Source: Talent Function Group LLC
Graphic by Alberto Cervantes/The Wall Street Journal

---

*This is called "a hiring funnel" or *yield model.* This one republished with permission of Dow Jones, Inc., from the *Wall Street Journal,* Lauren Weber, January 24, 2012, http://online.wsj.com/news/articles/SB10001424052970204624204577178941034941330; permission conveyed through Copyright Clearance Center, Inc.

You can be forgiven for feeling as though this resume of yours, this little emissary you're sending on ahead to plead your case for being given an interview, is having to make its way across a battlefield to safety, dodging bullets all the way. But I want to teach you how to dodge those bullets. You can alter the way you were going to set up, construct, and format your resume, as we shall see in the next chapter.

It helps if you keep in mind, throughout this process, that employers obviously don't just want to eliminate.

No, ultimately they want to *find*. Once human eyes are reviewing your resume, they are looking for certain positive things as they scan down your resume.

THE THREE THINGS EMPLOYERS ARE
HOPING TO FIND IN YOUR RESUME'S PAINTING OF YOU

Even during the elimination game, employers are keeping their eyes open for some things they really want. Good things. You need to know what these are. Obviously.

All generalizations we might make at this point are suspect. If someone tells you today that all employers are searching for employees who are kind, someone else will show you tomorrow an employer who is looking for someone tough as nails, who takes no prisoners.

So, generalizations are dangerous. Still, *in general* . . . there are three things employers are most hoping to find, as they glance at your resume.

And the first two are: Competence plus Compassion.

To expand that a bit, employers want to know if you can do the job, of course, but they also want to know, *How do you get along with people?*

Or put another way: they want to know, *What can you do? What do you know? What experience have you had?* But they also want to know, *What are your people skills?*

The latter are sometimes called your *soft skills.* "Soft" means "unquantifiable." It is kind of a silly term*—reminds you of softheaded—but there you have it.

If "soft" skills are so important, you naturally want to know what they are. Well, they range all over the map, but they are basically concerned with how you interact with people. Here's a brief list of some of them.

"SOFT SKILLS"**

You have good soft skills if you (*choose any or all*): are likable—friendly, cheerful, optimistic, open, honest, even-tempered, emotionally stable—and manage yourself well; are confident, conscientious, and dependable, with a sense of humor; interact well with coworkers and customers or

---

*See "There Is Nothing Soft About 'Soft Skills,'" *The Intentional Workplace,* October 28, 2010, intentionalworkplace.com/2010/10/28/there-is-nothing-soft-about-soft-skills.

**The term was apparently coined in 1985 by Wayne Payne in his *A Study of Emotion: Developing Emotional Intelligence,* and it started being used widely after the subject of emotional intelligence became more popular, due to Daniel Goleman publishing a series of books on that subject, beginning in 1995. Robert Sternberg's 1997 classic *Successful Intelligence* also demonstrated the importance of soft skills.

clients regardless of their background; can see things through others' eyes; are understanding, compassionate, empathetic, a good communicator, a good listener, a good learner, good at resolving conflicts, flexible, and adaptive; can stay calm, cool, and collected; have the ability to motivate others, not intimidate others. *Good soft skills* means you understand yourself and your own inner world and have a high "emotional intelligence quotient" (EQ).[*]

The one thing *soft* most assuredly does not mean is "a soft manager, going easy on people who fail to perform, tolerating mistakes from others, repeatedly."

So, to my point: everyone knows that employers are looking over your resume to see, *What can you do? What do you know? What experience have you had? What education?* What many job-hunters or career-changers do not know is that employers are also heavily focused on how you get along with people.

They want both, and I mean *both*; but they will privately confess to you that, for many jobs, they give priority to the question of how you get along with people. In the past, employees, especially managers, have wrecked a company because while they were very competent at what they did with information or things, they had terrible people skills. So, it's important to find this out *now.*

---

[*]Incidentally, by the by, you can take "free" online tests that claim to determine your emotional intelligence, on such sites as www.queendom.com. It takes quite a while to finish all 146 questions there, and then they want you to buy a report (for just under ten bucks) that will explain your score to you, and what areas you need to work on. (*Free?*) Anyway, most of you probably don't need or want this, but there you have it, just in case.

Aye, and there's the rub. Traditional resumes have a format that is designed to help you make the case for the first part of the equation—*what you can do, what you know, what experience you have had*—but that format is lousy at communicating anything about the second part of the equation: *how do you get along with people?*

That's where resumes come up short. We'll see, in a minute, what you can do about that.

But first, remember how I said there were three things, not just two, that employers are generally looking for when they glance at your resume? Well, here is the third thing:

Anything Disturbing.

Yes, when they're looking at the painting of you that the words on your resume are creating in their imagination, heaven help you if they notice a blemish or ugly gouge in your portrait that draws their attention and makes them shake their head.

In other words, this third thing is not about something you should put in; this is about something you should take great care to leave out.

I say it again: on your resume it is important to leave out *anything that will disturb them.* Such things *might* come up later, during an interview with them, once you get it; and if that happens, fine. You can explain it. But you don't want it on your resume—this piece of paper that they're only giving an eight-second look.

I know you may be wondering what I mean by "anything disturbing." Well, to understand that, we can do no better than to turn to the Internet.

GOOGLE IS YOUR NEW RESUME

If you're not on the Internet,* then you can just forget this whole section.**

But according to the latest survey, 85 percent of us in the United States are, via either home computer or smartphone.*** Not only on it, but conspicuously and frequently, leaving tracks behind. You know. Facebook. Twitter. Pinterest. Instagram, Tumblr, Google+, MySpace, Flickr, Picasa, Craigslist, eBay, YouTube, blogs, photos, LinkedIn, and much more.

Many of us, in fact, have left enough material about ourselves there to constitute the makings of a good resume, if we were to put it all together. And Google has.**** (*It's just not organized.*)

---

*If you are out of work for any length of time, and you do not have the skills of knowing how to use a computer or how to access the Internet, you will be wise beyond your years if you go take some computer courses at your local community college or adult school or your nearest CareerOneStop center (now called American Job Centers).

**According to surveys, all but 2 percent of the population *could* be on the Internet. That 2 percent live in nonwired rural areas. The main reason others are not? Age, cost, or no interest in it (www.theverge.com/2013/8/26/4660008/pew-study-finds-30-percent-americans-have-no-home-broadband).

***This according to the Pew Internet & American Life Project's May 2013 and April 2012 surveys; 80 percent of *households* have Internet access, but this average fluctuates (greatly!) according to annual income. Only 46 percent of adults have Internet access at home, if they live in households with annual income under $30,000. But 87 percent of adults have Internet access at home, if they live in households with annual income over $75,000. And 99 percent have Internet access at home if they live in households with annual income over $150,000.

****So has Safari, or Bing, or any of a dozen other search engines. For an October 1, 2013, list of Google's most popular rivals, see www.ebizmba.com/articles/search-engines.

Yes, if you are on the Internet you no longer have just one resume. You now have two, in effect, whether you want to (two) or not. Because employers nowadays look at both: the resume you carefully compose, then send to them, and the one that Google.com will randomly display before their eyes, when they type your name into Google's search engine and bammo! If you've been anywhere near the Internet—and as I said, most of us have—and if you've posted anything on Facebook, Twitter, and the like, or if you have your own website or webcasts or photo album or blog, or if you've been on anyone else's Facebook page, every aspect of you may be discovered by that employer.

All of this is subject, of course, to your privacy settings—who you allow to see your pages and who you don't—and *puhleeze*, an employer does not have the legal right to demand your password; if they do demand it, you've got to weigh how much you really want to work there. Unless you're desperate, you do have the right to refuse and go look elsewhere for a job.

Let us pause a moment to shed a tear over the death of the "good old days" when you had control over your private life when you went job-hunting. The only way an interviewer could learn much about you was from that piece of paper called your resume or CV. The good thing about this—from your point of view—was that you had absolute control over what went on that piece of paper. You could always show only your best side.

You could omit anything that was embarrassing, or anything from your past that you have long since regretted.

Short of their hiring a private detective, or talking to your previous employers, a prospective employer couldn't find out much else about you.

That was nice. But those days are gone forever. With social media sites, much of your life is now an open book. As Edward Snowden and a host of others have been reminding us, privacy is kinda dead.

It's easy now for anyone to find out more about you than just your resume.

So naturally, upon deciding to explore the resume you sent them, a vast majority of employers (91 percent of them, according to recent surveys*) will *Google* your name—*yes, Google has become both noun and verb*—before they'll consider interviewing you, or consider hiring you.

And what are they looking for? Well, as I said, they're looking for anything *disturbing*, in the total picture the Internet paints of you.

With Google they often find it: 70 percent of all employers who regularly Google a job-hunter's name have in fact found some thing that caused them to reject an applicant.

---

*As, for example, a study by Reppler.com, reported by Kashmir Hill in *Forbes* ("What Prospective Employers Hope to See in Your Facebook Account") on October 3, 2011.

What kinds of things? Well, the biggie is anything that shows you lied on your (other) resume. Experts say that 82 percent of all resumes need checking out, because there's something that looks questionable. When I first interviewed experts who fact-check resumes for companies, and heard this statistic, I thought it was way too large. Nope, turns out it wasn't. And isn't. Apparently, people lie, right and left, on their resumes these days—and think nothing of it—unless or until they get caught—and, consequently, don't get the interview or lose the job. Then, of course, it's too late. *So, don't . . . do . . . it!*

In addition to lies, there are some other things employers generally dislike: bad grammar or gross misspelling on your Facebook or LinkedIn profile; your using bad words (starting with "f . . . "); badmouthing of previous employers or people with whom you've worked; any signs of racism, prejudice, or jaw-dropping opinions; anything indicating alcohol or drug abuse; obsession with sex, as well as any—to put it delicately—*inappropriate content*, etc. Not to mention the general overall *tone* of you, on the Internet.

Remember, employers are looking for three things: competence, compassion, and . . . *nothing disturbing*. Don't just shrug your shoulders and ignore this last.

If they find something disturbing, they *will* dump you. You will never be called in. Or hired.

CLEANING UP YOUR GOOGLE "RESUME"

Not fair, you say. And I agree. But let's look at the bright side: you can fix this, if you will just give it some thought beforehand.

In almost all circumstances, you can manage or remove anything online that might disturb a prospective employer, prior to that employer's Googling you. Prior to your sending them your resume. In other words, you can *clean up* your portrait on the Internet.

First of all, there's an automated way to at least begin the process. The site is www.reppler.com. In a few minutes, it will go through all the sites you link it to—your Facebook, Twitter, LinkedIn, Flickr, Picasa, and YouTube accounts, and so forth—and then flag those things you might want to delete. Nice app! And so far, it's free. Use it.

Secondly, you can use your brains. *Naturally!*

Try painting an ideal but realistic picture of yourself, in your own mind, that you'd like the employer to see, or imagine, when they Google you. Paint that picture in broad strokes, by making a list of adjectives you'd hope would pop into the employer's mind when they look you up.

Experienced? Professional? Determined? Creative? Organized? Well-rounded? Honest? Trustworthy? Kind?

Make your own realistic list. It should include, above all, any of the soft skills we saw on pages 18–19 that you feel you can legitimately, honestly claim as your own.

That list is how you'd like to come across, on the Internet.

Now Google yourself and read everything the search engine pulls up about you, most especially on social sites like Facebook, LinkedIn, Plaxo, MySpace, Tumblr, Craigslist, Pinterest, or YouTube.

Remove anything you posted, or allowed others to post, that contradicts the items on that list of yours.

How? Just type or speak the following into a search engine like Google: "How to remove an item from [here name the site you are concerned about; say, Facebook]," and the chances are 9 out of 10 that Google will point you to *somebody's* clever detailed, step-by-step instructions for "scrubbing" that site.

Just remember, you want *current* instructions, so look at the date on the list of items the search engine pops up. Pick the most recent, and try what they suggest.

As you're doing this cleanup, if you come across any sites (LinkedIn, in particular) that allow you to fill out a profile, *STOP!* and *DO IT.* Fill it out completely. Now. These "profiles" are little mini-resumes. So, show them great care. Cross every t, and dot every i, and have someone check your spelling. And grammar. Particularly if English isn't your first language. Leave no part of the profile blank unless you have a very good reason.

More than 277 million people are on LinkedIn alone, and it is the first place an experienced employer turns to, on the Internet, when they are curious about you.[*]

---

[*]If you want to keep up to date with these kinds of statistics, Digital Marketing Ramblings (http://expandedramblings.com) is your go-to site.

If you're on LinkedIn, you can find guidance about filling out your profile at http://blog.linkedin.com/2012/02/14/ profile-completeness. They emphasize that you should include the following:

1. A profile photo, head and shoulders, broadly smiling. Yes, do it. Surveys reveal that employers spend 19 percent of their time on your LinkedIn mini-resume just looking at your picture.*

2. Your industry and location (*postal code at least*).

3. An up-to-date description of your current position (if you're presently employed; otherwise, your most recent one).

4. Two past positions at least; if you choose to list all the jobs or positions you've held, do so in reverse chronological order (working backward), along with descriptions of your roles.

5. At least five of your favorite and best skills.

6. Your education (where you went to school).

7. A summary about yourself.

8. At least fifty connections (LinkedIn will tell you how).

---

*Will Evans, "Eye Tracking Online Metacognition: Cognitive Complexity and Recruiter Decision Making," *The Ladders*, 2012, http://cdn.theladders.net/static/ images/basicSite/pdfs/TheLadders-EyeTracking-StudyC2.pdf.

If you're on Twitter, fill out your profile there, too. Find out how at www.dummies.com/how-to/content/how-to-complete-your-twitter-profile-settingso.html.

And looking down the road, *be sure* you make it a weekly or monthly practice to keep such mini-resumes up to date. *Really* up to date. I know that's hard, but you do want to look professional, and there is nothing that makes you look less professional than having an obviously outdated profile, somewhere, somehow.

Okay now, I've been talking about the Internet as though it's a potential millstone around your neck. Actually, if you do things right, it can become a tremendous asset instead. All you have to do is just make your two "resumes"—*what you write* plus *what Google turns up*—work in tandem with one another.

MAKING YOUR TWO RESUMES WORK TOGETHER

Let's go back to our earlier problem: I said that although employers' eyes, looking at our resume, want to find out not only if we are competent but also if we have compassion, it turns out to be incredibly difficult if not impossible for them to determine the latter. A resume's traditional form and nature just doesn't allow that.

We know this, and we want to help them. But just when we are at our wit's end about how to fix this, along comes our Google resume to the rescue. It offers us a chance to correct that little problem, because it is there that we can triumph over the limits of a traditional resume. There, on the Internet, we can demonstrate and parade our people skills.

And if we commit to doing that, does it actually work? Yes, it sure does. Some 68 percent of employers have hired a candidate because they were impressed by what Google showed them about that candidate's skills with people, in addition to their creativity or professionalism demonstrated online, and the wide range of interests exhibited.*

The chart on page 30 gives an overview of how your two resumes complement each other, in painting a picture of You in the imagination of an employer.

Thus Google supplements your traditional resume. And your traditional resume, in turn, supplements Google. It's no quick matter for an employer to Google you. The stuff about you that Google can call up may be all over the map.

You help by using your written resume to summarize and organize the most pertinent information about yourself, as it relates to this employer's needs and job requirements.

---

*According to a www.reppler.com study, reported by Kashmir Hill in *Forbes* ("What Prospective Employers Hope to See in Your Facebook Account") on October 3, 2011.

TYPE OF RESUME:	1. TRADITIONAL RESUME	2. GOOGLE "RESUME"
ORIGIN	Created by you or your agent	Gathered by search engine
PRIMARY FOCUS IS ON:	Your technical skills (what you can do, what you know, what experience you've had)	Your people skills ("soft skills"): your relationship to and handling of people (as shown on Facebook, etc.)
SECONDARY EMPHASIS ON:	Your people skills	Your technical skills
FORM OF THE INFORMATION:	Well organized	A mish-mash
SIDE OF THE BRAIN APPEALED TO:	Left side of the brain	Right side of the brain
NATURE OF THE INFORMATION:	Evidence, with stories	Impressions
WAYS OF IMPROVING THIS RESUME:	Experience: Cite more stories, even if in one brief sentence, to prove you are not just *claiming* you have this technical skill or that, but you actually have demonstrated you have that skill.	Anecdotes: Put up more stories, on your Facebook page and elsewhere, which show you are likable and good with people. (Tell stories of times when you demonstrated any of the soft skills on pages 18–19.)

SUMMARY

Well, this is the end of your preparation. What have we learned thus far?

1. You are not primarily a writer, but a painter when you create a resume. You're writing words. But employers have imaginations. They can't help themselves. Your words inevitably create a picture of yourself in their imagination. So, you must think of your words as giant paintbrushes.

2. You have two resumes, loosely speaking: the one you write (or "paint") *and* the one that Google pulls together about you. With these two working in tandem, you can convey to an employer the two things they most want to know: that you are competent but also compassionate. Your resume alone can't do much about the "compassionate" part—your soft skills, your people skills. But your postings on the Internet, done thoughtfully and intentionally, can complement your resume's focus on only your technical skills.

3. You must take especial care, on both "resumes," to remove anything that an employer might find disturbing, when they are weighing whether or not to invite you in for an interview.

4. Employers play the Elimination Game before they play the Hiring Game. Your resume therefore doesn't at all get the attention you feel it deserves. On average, it's eight seconds. You must therefore structure your resume so that it paints a quick impression of who you are in the top third of that resume, using key words.

5. As part of the Elimination Game, ATS technology may be used to run your resume through an automatic scanning (and possible rejection) procedure, at large companies. But hiring is not all about large companies. In fact, 66 percent of all jobs in the United States are with small companies, having fewer than 250 employees. There, your resume is most likely dealing with human eyes from the beginning (*go back to number one*).

Now, with this preparation, you are ready to write that resume.

2 HOW TO CONSTRUCT A WINNING RESUME

DECISION #1: WHO SHOULD WRITE IT: THEM, OR ME?

I. THEM

"Them" of course are professional resume writers. There's a whole tribe of them out there. They are in virtually every town and village in the United States. They even have an association, called the National Résumé Writers' Association, and they get together annually. If you aren't good at writing a resume, they will do it for you. For a fee. Of course. That's how they make their living. Their prices vary. Greatly. As to why, see http://blog.knockemdead.com/2011/08/resume-is-critical-marketing-tool-for.html, written by Martin Yate, an immensely popular and knowledgeable career expert.

If you decide you want to hire a professional resume writer, go to www.thenrwa.com/whyhireaprofessionalresumewriter. Or consult your local Yellow Pages, either online or off. You should briefly interview at least two or three of them and then back home *compare* them, before deciding to hire one of them.

Compare? What are you looking for? Well—surprise, surprise—the same thing an employer is looking for in you: *competence* plus *compassion*.

Compassion is easy to tell. Do they feel like people anxious to help anyone who is in trouble, regardless of income; or do they seem to be more interested in making money, serving primarily high-paying clients? (*Yes, Virginia, the tribe is large, and it takes all kinds to make a world.*) Yes, "the laborer is worthy of his hire," but you also want compassion!

As for their competence, there are four degrees or levels:

Competency Level #1. They will claim they can create a beautifully written document for you.

Critique: No surprise here; "writer" is in their very name. Of course, that doesn't mean the resume they write for you will go anywhere, but at least it will look beautiful.

Competency Level #2. They will claim their resume can "sell you" to employers. This is a common claim, in the trade.

Critique: Many of the resume writers who operate at this level were marketers in another life, and can produce some stunning sales pieces.* But no matter what *they* may tell

---

*Many of them were indebted to Jay Conrad Levinson, author of the best-selling Guerrilla Marketing series of books, from 1984 until his death on October 10, 2013.

you, no matter what all your *friends* may tell you, no matter what the *world* may tell you, it is not a resume's job to sell you. That task has to be saved for the interview.

What *can* a resume do? Pique an employer's curiosity? Sure. Intrigue an employer? Maybe so. But actually cause employers to hire you, just on the basis of this sales piece, without even an interview? Hardly ever, unless it's a digital design, marketing, or sales position you're going for. And often not even then. An employer buys a *person*, not a *pamphlet.*

Competency Level #3. They will claim their resume can get you invited in for an interview with some employers.

Critique: Well, that is a resume's true vocation, so if the resume they write for you actually does that, theirs is a high level of competence.

Competency Level #4. They will claim their resume can get you invited in for an interview with a particular target (employer) of your own choice, a place where you're dying to work.

Critique: A lot of people claim this, but it's often empty words. However, if it turns out to be true, then Bingo! This is the highest level of competence you can find, among resume writers. This resume writer is *really good* at what they do.

So much for competencies. Now to the $64,000 question: If you are comparing two or three resume writers, how can you tell which level of competence each writer has?

Well, here is a clue: as I've been emphasizing, a resume has a mission, and anticipates a result. If you hire someone to write your resume for you, you want it to result in your getting in for an interview.

If the resume writer you are considering hiring is results-oriented, they will know that, and they will have kept track of their results.

So, did they? You have a right to ask: *What percentage of your clients actually got an interview because of the resume you wrote for them? Say, in the last three months?*

If they are good, they will know. If they are honest, they will tell you.[*]

Many won't know. It has just never occurred to them to keep track of the results.

Others know, but will not tell you (you can probably guess why).

I once visited a noted resume writer in a distant city from where I lived. We'll call her "Ms. Betty." I walked in the office door, and found myself in an outer reception area. "I'd like to talk to Ms. Betty," I said. "I'm doing some research."

"She's busy," said the front desk person, "but I can answer any question you have."

"Okay," I said, "I'm doing some research, and I'm trying to find out what percentage of a resume writer's clients actually

---

[*]There are in fact resume writers or firms (www.getinterviews.com is one example) who make this their condition for their fee.

got an interview as a result of their resume, during the last three months. I know of Ms. Betty's reputation, so I'm hoping she can help me."

The woman at the front desk looked stricken; you would think I had asked her for her bank account number. "I'll get Ms. Betty, right away," she said.

Ms. Betty immediately appeared, and then spent a lot of time trying to convince me that the statistic was irrelevant. "I write beautiful resumes," she said, "that is enough."

No, no, no, it's not!

If you pay a dentist to fill a cavity, you want that cavity filled; not just a nice-looking cap placed on top of the still-open cavity. *Ouch!* Beauty is nice to have. But in the world of job-hunting, only results count.

II. ME

Okay, let's suppose you can't (or don't want to) pay the cost of getting someone to write your resume for you. You're going to do it on your own. Any way to get some free guidance?

Good news: There are indeed online sites that will (figuratively speaking) hold your hand and walk you through the task of writing your own resume, step by step. A nice list of them can be found at http://jobsearch.about.com/od/resumebuildersites/Resume_Builder_Sites.htm. These resume-building services on the Internet are mostly free.

Good. Grand to have them.

Not to be a wet blanket or anything, though, may I add just a tiny word of caution here?

Just because websites *say* they're free doesn't mean they are. Resume writers, by and large, are nice people with good hearts. But in addition to some among them who are just inept, there are also crooks in their midst, wolves in sheep's clothing. *Crooks!*

I've learned about them from my friends in states' attorneys general offices. Also, the U.S. president's Advisor for Consumer Affairs some years ago asked me to write a white paper for them, describing all the tricks that crooks play on job-hunters, with resumes and other parts of the job-hunt. The Federal Trade Commission then read that paper and called me to Washington, to dig deeper. During our mutual exchange, they shared additional tricks and traps they had discovered that I hadn't run across—'til then. The total picture—theirs plus mine—was truly depressing. Why do crooks decide to prey on people when they are most vulnerable—i.e., out of work, unemployed, and desperate? I don't know.*

What I do know is, you must be vigilant. It is not likely you will run into a crook, but keep the possibility in the back of your mind, so that if you turn to some "free" site or company on the Internet for help with your resume or whatever, and that "free" site suddenly asks for your credit card midway through, *stop!*

---

*The one writer I know of that makes it his business to expose these kinds of scams is Nick Corcodilos, at AskTheHeadhunter.com.

Scam Alert!

The favorite scam of crooks in this field involves claiming their services are free, then revealing—deep into the process—that there is a small charge for this or that, and therefore they need your credit card number now, to cover that small fee. Except, somewhere there in the small print—very, very small print—it says that you are giving them authorization to charge your credit card monthly. Which they then do, hoping you won't notice. And you very well may not, unless you examine your credit card bill in scrupulous detail every month. (They often use a name you won't recognize.)

So, if any site suddenly asks for your credit card, study the teeny-tiny print on the site, word for word. You might also want to look up that site, company, or person on www.ripoffreport.com and see if there are any complaints about their financial practices. If after all this you *just have a feeling*, it just doesn't smell right, I know you're a very kind person, but please, *do not* give them the benefit of the doubt.

Bail.

Immediately.

Go find guidance elsewhere. Heaven knows, there are enough books, articles, blogs, and YouTube guides to give you lots of advice as you set about doing this.

Can you write your resume yourself?

Maybe.

Maybe not.

But before you hire someone, first at least *try* writing it yourself.

Many people are surprised to discover they can. With just a little guidance, and with their best friend checking them for grammar and spelling, afterward.

And if so, wonderful. The real *You* will come across much clearer. Your resume will be professional looking, one hopes, but it will also come across as personal, if you did the writing in your own words.

Some employers value the personal touch, particularly those at *small companies* (250 or fewer employees).

So, write away.

Just keep this in mind—the first rule in writing your own resume is: *Don't lie.*

Ever.

About anything.

The second rule is: *Don't lie.*

And the third rule is: *Don't lie.*

Your resume must paint a portrait of yourself in the imagination of the employer who reads your resume. But it must be an honest portrait.

In this day and age, if you lie about something, it will come out!

DECISION #2: LEFT UP ON THE VILLAGE GREEN, OR ON SOMEBODY'S DOORSTEP?

What do you put in your resume? What kind of picture do you paint of yourself, in the imagination of the employer who reads it? The answer is a strange one: *your resume's content is determined by how you're going to distribute it, once written.* Here's how it works:

I. LEFT UP ON THE VILLAGE GREEN

Is it your intent to—metaphorically speaking—walk your resume down to the village green, and nail it to a tree there, for all passersby to see? (*Or if you have no village green, then to its digital equivalents: Monster. Careerbuilder. Dice. Indeed. Simply Hired. Craigslist. And the like. Same distribution, but nailed to a digital tree.*)

There is no specific target, just any employer in your field.

It's equivalent to writing a letter that begins with *To Whom It May Concern.*

If this *is* your intent, then you write a generic resume highlighting why you're a wonderful worker. With evidence.

Period. End of story.

Here, the resume is mainly about You. *"Here's all I have done, thus far, in my life."*

It's like drawing, with your words, a full-on portrait of your whole face. You're hoping some employer in your field—any employer who has a vacancy—will come across your resume, decide you sound really interesting, and call you in.

That's one type of content. Dictated, as I said, by how you're going to distribute your resume.*

We'll call this your General Resume (some call it your Master Resume).

II. ON SOMEBODY'S DOORSTEP

Or is it your intent, instead, to target individual employers with your resume, addressing them by name and posting your resume on their front door, as it were; which is to say, on their website, or via LinkedIn, or mailed directly to them? In that case, the content of your resume must specifically revolve around that employer, or—to be more exact—that employer's job requirements.

It's a tailor-made resume, and if you're targeting five different employers, or five different job openings, then you write five different resumes, basically identical at their core, but varying when it comes down to details.

---

*There is, of course, a third type of distribution; namely, no distribution. You just write your resume, and then keep it to yourself, at the ready—as it were—for that day when you need it. This is most typically done by those who are gainfully employed at present. In form, however, it is identical to the resume I have just been mentioning. Generic. *To Whom It May Concern.* All about You. Full-faced portrait.

Here we have a different type of content from the first.

This type of resume is equivalent to writing a personal letter addressed to a particular individual.

In this case the resume is mainly about *Them*.

It is *their* needs, *their* goals, *their* challenges that you focus your resume on, talking about yourself only insofar as it shows that you are hopefully a good fit with those things.

If they've posted a vacancy, you begin with the key words they used, in describing who they're looking for, and then in your resume you allude to each of those words, one by one, citing how you match that key word.

If they haven't posted any vacancy, then you research that organization (which is to say, you Google them) and find out what kinds of skills and knowledges they have always seemed to hunger for, in their ads or postings in the past. And then in your resume you allude to each of them, one by one, plus how you match those requirements.

In the end, your resume here mentions only the experience, skills, and knowledge you have that are relevant to a job at that place. It's like a painting of only the side of your face—your best side—tilted toward them. No need to show them the rest.

We'll call this your Targeted Resume.

Now you see what I mean when I say your resume's content is determined, strangely enough, by how you're going to distribute it. You must decide *that* first, before you ever start writing.

DECISION #3: EMPTY CLAIMS, OR CONCRETE EVIDENCE?

I. EMPTY CLAIMS

When you start writing your resume, your first concern will likely be: What should you include?

But, given that your resume is first going to go through the Elimination Game, before it can participate in the Hiring Game, your first concern should be, What should you leave out? What words should you *not* use?

You see, there are certain words that—if they see them on a resume—make employers scream: *Not again!!*

I think you will be surprised to learn what they are. Some of them are the very words you were probably planning on using in your resume. You were thinking that if you sprinkled some of these "magic" words around, this would make your resume more attractive to employers.

Un-uh. There is broad consensus that they have just the opposite effect on the majority of employers and HR people.

Here are the *"no longer magic"* words, the words that make most employers scream:

Able, *accustomed to fast-paced environments*, analytical, *approximately*, assisted with, *attempted*, bottom-line focused, *capable*, career objective, *confident*, creative, *demonstrating a talent for*, dependable, *driven*, dynamic, *excellent*, effective leader, *energetic*, exceeded expectations, *exceptional*, experienced, *expert*, extensive experience with, *familiar with*, fast learner, *flexible*, goal oriented, *good at*, good (or excellent) communication skills, *contributed to*, go-to person, *4.0 GPA*, hard worker, *has talent for*, highly qualified, *highly skilled*, innovative, *looking for a challenging opportunity*, loyal,   *outside-the-box thinker*, outstanding, *participated in*, perfectionist, *people person*, proactive, *problem solver*, professional, *proven ability*, proven track record, *references furnished upon request*, reliable, *responsible for*, results-oriented, *quick learner*, responsible for, *results focused*, scalable, *salary negotiable*, seasoned, *self-starter*, skilled, *strong*, strong work ethic, *successfully*, suitable, *team player*, top-flight, *top-notch*, track record, *workaholic*, works well under pressure, *works well with all levels*.

"You're kidding. What could possibly be wrong with those words?"

In many cases, nothing.

The first time they were used in a resume.

They looked *grand*.

But now that employers have seen them five thousand times on five thousand resumes, the words have been drained of all meaning. Employers and their HR people use four words to describe *why they're fed up* with seeing these words.

Cliché. Buzzword. Hyperbole. Outdated.

Ask them to expand on these four words, and they will quote their dictionaries to say that by and large these are words that are meant to sound important, intended to impress, but they have long since lost their originality or force through overuse, so that now they have become meaningless due to endless repetition of one word or another by job-hunter after job-hunter after job-hunter after job-hunter.

Outdated? Yes, some of them. Once upon a time they were found on every resume, but now they are regarded as passé. "Career objective" is one of them. That is rarely wanted on today's resumes. "Salary negotiable" for another. And "references furnished upon request" for yet another. Fashions change, even in resumes.

The overarching major problem with these words is that most employers consider them to be just empty claims, devoid of any proof.

"You say you're able, analytical, bottom-line focused, capable, creative, effective, exceptional, experienced, expert, goal oriented, highly qualified, highly skilled, innovative, outstanding, problem solver, professional, results-oriented, seasoned, self-starter, skilled, top-flight, and top-notch? Prove it! Give me numbers, percentages, illustrations, or substantiation."

Employers have been fooled in the past by these words. "Outstanding," for example, sounded impressive, but it just didn't hold up, once that person was hired.

So employers are tired of these words now. Unless they are backed up.

These days employers want evidence. On your resume. Before they'll call you in. As I said, they want numbers, percentages, illustrations. That sort of thing.

Try it! These "used-to-be-magic words" can often be redeemed by expansion, and a number. Example:

"Experienced" (*Blah*)

"Experienced technician" (*Just okay*)

"Experienced wind turbine technician" (*Better*)

"Experienced wind turbine technician with 8 years experience on California wind farms" (*Now you're talkin'.*)

That's the kind of thing employers are looking for!!

II. CONCRETE EVIDENCE

What kind of evidence are employers (in general) looking for, on your resume, that proves you can do what you claim you can do?

Usually it's experience that they're looking for.

Length of time counts, too. If you've done it for seven years, that carries more weight than if you've just done it for two months. *How long ago* you did it matters, too. That's why it's important to include dates on your resume (e.g., *2005–2013*).

Numbers are the most important evidence of all. Employers want to make money. You are a cost. They want to know if the money you make for them, or the money you save them, will exceed your cost. They'd even like to guess by how much. Giving them figures regarding your past achievements helps them to gauge that.

They're looking for things like: *"During my seven years there, I sold a million dollars' worth of merchandise each year,"* or *"I increased sales by 23 percent."* Or *"I was able to reduce costs so that we could undersell our chief competitor by $34 per item, resulting in a profit of $75,000 the first year."* Or *"I invented a new procedure that cut the waiting time by 2 hours."* Or *"Due to my care in fitting the customer, returns dropped to only 3 per month; they were running 39 a month, on average, before I came."*

DECISION #4: YOU ARE A COST OR YOU ARE A PROFIT

Generally speaking, employers are more reluctant to hire these days than they were before 2008. If they can get by with the workforce they already have, they will. Given an economy that is taking way too long to get back to normal. Given the uncertainties about the future, due to our dysfunctional Congress. Given the as-yet-unclear implications of the Affordable Care Act. Given the effects of raising the minimum wage. Employers are more reluctant to hire, these days.

Sometimes they will dip their toe in the waters. They will advertise a vacancy and interview candidates just to see if hiring more workers seems to make sense. But often, even during the interviews, they are not yet sure. They're waiting to be impressed. They're waiting to be convinced.

If they decide yes, then they face the big question: shall I hire part-time or full-time? More and more, across the board, their answer is part-time. Even when, prior to 2008, their answer would have been: *full-time, of course.*

You must be prepared for this.

To figure out *how*, let's step back for a moment. Suppose we lived in a different world altogether. A world without resumes. You're at a meeting of some kind, and find yourself accidentally sitting next to the person you would most like to work for, in the whole world. And she—or he—is friendly and willing to chat. You discover that they are weighing whether or not to hire someone.

The direction of the conversation is up to you. What would you want to talk about?

I expect you'd be curious. Curious, initially, to know what the job involves. What would be the tasks, projects, deadlines, expectations, goals this new worker would be assigned, and who would they be working with?

Then if you liked the sound of what you'd heard, you'd want a chance to argue gently why you'd be the perfect person for this job.

Except you wouldn't just say it that way—"Hey, I'm the best." A little arrogant-sounding, put that way. No, you'd say the same thing but in their language, the language of almost every organization in the world: money.

Every organization needs money, even if they're a nonprofit. So, you'd want to show them how you'd bring in more money, or save them more money, than the cost of hiring you would add up to. You'd want to show them how you would represent a profit for them, not just a cost. That is far more persuasive than "Hey, I'm the best."

That's what you'd do in a different world. Now back to this world. It is not so easy to chat with an employer, but you do have a resume at your command. So the $64,000 question (again) is, How do you write your resume so it conveys the fact that if they'd hire you, you'd represent a profit for them, and not merely a cost?

Ideally, you'd like to be able to quote actual numbers—something like, *My salary and perks would cost you $85,000 a year, but I have figured out a way to save you (or make you) $260,000 over a year's time, once I'm up and running.*

Ending with: *So—$260,000 minus $85,000—I represent a profit for you, not a cost.*

If the employer reading your resume was sitting on the fence about whether to hire some new blood, or not, this would push them into the *Yes* column. You've said you're the best, but in their language: money.

Problem: Nine hundred and ninety-nine times out of a thousand you won't be able to quote numbers as I have just fantasized.

So, what *can* you do?

You can write your resume so it demonstrates that this is the chief thing you have on your mind when you're looking for *any* job: how can I be a profit there, rather than just a cost?

You convey this by focusing on words like: *accomplished (and say what)*, accomplishments included, *time saved,* any increased profits, *any reduction in costs,* any breaking existing sales record, *created,* created new, *developed,* example, *improved,* increased, *increased productivity by X percent,* initiated cost-saving, *ranked first in sales,* pioneered new incentive program, *reduced,* researched, *reduced costs by,* secured five new x worth $x, *won,* under budget by. . . .

And—well, you get the point. *How can I be a profit, and not just a cost,* should underlie every thought you have, every line you write, every bold stroke you paint, on your resume.

With all the above words, you want to throw in any NUMBERS, any PERCENTAGES, and—assuming this is a Targeted Resume—any details that look transferable from where you were, to where you want to be.

And make the connection for them. "In a company that, like yours, had less than a hundred employees, I was able to . . ." Or "In an organization that, like yours, was facing a marked decrease in sales, I was able to . . ."

It does not always appear easy to say how you represented a profit to your employers in the past. So, let's look at some examples that may offer you a guide.

1. Think of some mythical person they might have hired who would have done that job very badly.

Compared to you, how much more would that person have cost them? For example, *let's say you paint houses, and your paint jobs last ten years. If they had hired someone who did a poor job, instead of you, how soon would they have had to have the house repainted? You know your industry well enough to know how long a shoddy paint job would have lasted, but let's guess here, and say it might have been five years; then the house owner would have had the whole cost again, plus inflation. So you can fairly say, "I did the painting so well that I typically saved my clients $x," where "x" is the cost of that second paint job, necessitated in just five years because of the shoddy job such a person would have done in the first place. To make the figure more impressive, you can make it a yearly sum: add up how many house paintings you did in a year—let's say it's "y." Then multiply "x" by "y" to get "z," and say, "In a year I typically saved my customers the total sum of 'z.'" That's no lie!*

2. Did you save the organization time, and thus increase their profit?* Either by accomplishing more work in less time than your predecessor had, or by meeting impossible deadlines and always saving the organization a penalty, or by

---

*These last three questions here are adapted, with permission, from original material written by Karin Abarbanel for the National Association for Female Executives, now out of print.

taking on additional responsibilities so that they didn't need to hire an additional (part-time) person? Put a guesstimate or number on all of these, if you can.

3. Did you save the organization money, and thus increase their profit? Either by finishing a major job (or project) below budget, while others would have gone over the budget, or by coming up with some true cost-saving ideas with respect to procedures they had always done "the old way"? Put a guesstimate or number on these if you can.

4. Did you increase the organization's total sales, and thus increase their profit? Either by attracting new customers or clients, or by generating new business, or by alerting the organization to a problem they were missing that could be easily solved, or by pointing out an opportunity or new market that they were missing? Put a guesstimate or number on all of these, if you can.

Now, I guarantee you that average job-hunters do not try to present themselves as a potential profit to the organization they send their resume to. "Salary negotiable" is a common phrase on resumes. That means they're thinking of themselves as a cost, and trying to soften the blow.

You represent a profit. Keep that always in your mind.

DECISION #5: JUST START WRITING, OR FIRST COLLECT ALL YOUR INFORMATION

A popular song many years ago began "I'm gonna sit right down and write myself a letter . . ." This is the approach some of us consider when it comes to crafting a resume. "I'm gonna sit right down and write . . ."

Sometimes that's a virtue. Most times that's a mistake.

When it's a virtue, it's because you already have a clear picture in your head of what an employer will be looking for. You will know from studies that in the first four seconds their eyes are scanning the top third of your resume for three things:[*]

1. **Your previous job titles**, with an explanation after each, in parentheses, if the meaning of that title isn't immediately obvious.

2. **The companies or organizations** where you have worked, and your starting and ending dates there, listed in reverse chronological order, working backward from the most recent.

3. **Your education**—just your degree and institution—plus any *relevant* additional training you have had

---

[*]Dr. John Sullivan, "Why You Can't Get a Job . . . Recruiting Explained by the Numbers," *ERE*, May 20, 2013, www.ere.net/2013/05/20/why-you-cant-get-a-job-recruiting-explained-by-the-numbers.

between then and now. If your education was
long ago, and you are concerned your age will be
held against you, omit any dates.

So, if you want to just start writing, you will write out those
three bits of information. Writing freely, writing loosely,
enjoying the ride, then going back later to edit and tighten
it up. Your right brain will have a ball.

BEFORE WRITING, CAST A WIDE NET

For most of us, however, our memory isn't so hot, so we will
profit from a more left brain approach, systematically gathering any information from our past that could possibly be
useful, before we actually begin writing.*

The Starter Kit here is designed to help you do this—so try
to fill it out thoroughly and systematically:**

A STARTER KIT OF 45+ QUESTIONS

Begin by thinking of the skills with information, or with
things, or with people, that you believe you possess innately,
or have picked up along the way. What things have you done
in your life or work experience that no one else has done, in
quite the same way? That last phrase is important.

---

*About "your past": Counselors who don't like resumes sardonically refer to
them as "obituaries."

**I have adapted this, with the written permission of my friend Tom O'Neil, from
an original document of his, which was and is copyright protected under the
New Zealand Copyright Act (1994) © cv.co.nz 2001. You should contact Tom at
www.cv.co.nz before you reproduce it, to get his consent.

Which achievements are you proud of? More to the point, which skills do you love? Take some blank sheets of paper and fill in any answers that occur to you.

As I mentioned in the last section, it is important to be quantitative when you talk about the results (e.g., mention dates, percentages, dollars, money or time saved, brand names, etc.).

Volunteer, Community, and Unpaid Work

1. Have you completed any voluntary or unpaid work for any organization or company? (e.g., church, synagogue, mosque, school, community service, or special needs organization)? If so, what?

Educational

2. Did you work while you were studying? If so, did you receive any promotions or achievements in that role?

3. Did you gain any scholarships?

4. Were you involved in any committees, etc.?

5. Did you win any awards for study?

6. Did you have any high (e.g., A or A+) grades? If so, what were the subjects—and grades? You may or may not decide to mention these on your actual resume.

Sales or Account Management

Have you ever been in sales? If so, what were some of your achievements? For example:

7. Have you ever consistently exceeded your set budget in that role? If so, by what percent or dollar value?

8. Have you exceeded your set budget in a particular month(s)/quarter(s) in a role? If so, by what percent or dollar value?

9. What level were you, compared to other sales professionals in your company? (e.g., "Number three out of twenty on the sales team")

10. Have you ever increased market share for your company? If so, by what percent or dollar value?

11. Have you ever brought in any major clients to your company?

12. What major clients are/were you responsible for managing and selling to?

13. Did you ever manage to generate repeat business or increase current business? If so, by what percent or dollar value?

14. Have you won any internal or external sales awards?

15. Did you develop any new successful promotional or marketing ideas that increased sales?

Administration, Customer Service, and Accounts

Have you ever been in customer service or helped run a business unit? If so, which of the following four things did you do:

16. Did you assist in reducing customer complaints, etc.?

17. Did you set up or improve any systems and/or processes?

18. Was there a quantifiable difference in the company or business unit when you first joined the business or project and when you completed the project or left the business?

19. Did you take any old administration or paperwork-based systems and convert them into an IT-based system?

Responsibility

20. Have you ever been responsible for the purchase of any goods or services in some job? (e.g., air travel or PC acquisition)

21. Have you ever had any budget responsibility? If so, to what level? (e.g., "Responsible for division budget of $500,000 per annum")

22. Have you ever been responsible for any staff over-sight? If so, in what capacity and/or how many staff members were you responsible for?

23. Were you responsible for any official or unofficial training? If so, what type, for whom, and how many people have you trained? (e.g., "Responsible for training twelve new staff in customer service as well as in using the in-house computer system")

24. Were you responsible for any official or unofficial coaching or mentoring of other staff?

Events or Conference Planning or Logistical Management

25. Have you organized any events or conferences? If so, how large were they (both people attending and total budget if possible) and where and when was the event(s) held?

26. Have you been involved in any major relocation projects?

27. Have you had responsibility with regard to any major suppliers? If so, who?

Computers

28. What systems, software, and hardware experience do you have? Desktop, notebook, mobile, smart-phones? Mac OS, Android, or Windows? Are you on LinkedIn, Plaxo, Twitter, Facebook, YouTube, etc., and if so how deep an expertise do you have with any of these sites? Use? Training people?

29. What software have you developed? Mobile apps? Systems software? What code have you written? Or what software are you an expert in using, or teaching?

30. Have you developed any start-ups? If so, what were they, and did they achieve your goals and/or success? What did you do digitally that positively affected any business you were doing?

31. Were you involved in any special computer-related projects that were outside of your job description?

Mechanical

32. Have you had experience on any kinds of machinery or equipment? What types and for how many years? What computerized automatic control systems, such as HVAC, are you familiar with?

33. If you ever worked on transportation devices, what were the airplane, farm equipment, truck, car, machine, or bike brands that you serviced, maintained, or repaired?

Building, Construction, Electrical, and Plumbing

34. If you ever worked in those fields, were there any major projects you worked on or completed? How much did the project(s) cost? (e.g., "Reception refurbishment—ABC Bank [Auckland Central Head Office] $1.2m")

General

35. How long have you spent within any field industry? (e.g., "Twelve years' experience within the fashion industry") List them all.

36. Were you promoted in any of your roles? If so, in what years and to which roles?

37. Was extra authority awarded to you after a period of time within a role? (*e.g.,* "Commenced as receptionist; then, after three months, awarded by being given further clerical responsibilities including data entry and accounts payable") It is not necessary that these responsibilities awarded to you should have changed your job title and/or salary.

38. Have you been asked to take part in, or lead, any trainee management courses or management development programs?

39. Were you asked to get involved in any special projects outside your job description? Or, did you ever volunteer for such? What was the result?

Positive Feedback

40. Have you ever received any client, customer, or managerial written commendations or letters of praise?

41. Can you think of any occasions where you gave excellent customer service? If so, how did you know the customer was satisfied? (Also: What was the outcome? How did it benefit the company?)

42. Did you receive any awards within your company or industry? (e.g., "Acknowledged for support or service of clients or staff, etc.")

Memberships

43. Have you been a representative on any committees (e.g., health and safety committee)? Any special responsibilities there?

44. Do you belong or have you belonged to any national associations, or to any local professional groups such as Toastmasters, Lions, or Rotary?

Published or Presented Work

45. Have you had any articles, papers, or features published in any magazines, journals, or books? If so, what publications and when? Have you written any books? Have you presented any topics at any conferences or completed any public speaking? If so, what subjects have you talked about and how large was the audience? List in detail.

- What value do you think you would add to a potential employer's business? How would you be "a resource" or even "a resource broker" for them, rather than just "a job beggar"? How would you be a profit, rather than just a cost? What kind of problems are you good at solving?

- In what ways do you think you stand out compared to other applicants who might have about the same qualifications as you have?

Okay, that concludes the outline. That should give you a good start. Modify the outline any way you want to—add items and questions to it, change the wording. Whatever.

Now it's time to boil all that information down to its essence. Now, it's time to start writing.

DECISION #6: POSTPONE YOUR WRITING, OR START WRITING NOW

Sure, you can just sit down at your computer keyboard, pull up Microsoft Word, and let your thoughts freely flow.

That's the way we used to do it. It came out looking something like this (on the next page):

E-J DYER   STREET, CITY, ZIP   TELEPHONE NO.

I SPEAK THE
LANGUAGE OF
MEN, MACHINERY,
AND MANAGEMENT . . .

OBJECTIVE

Sales of Heavy Equipment

QUALIFICATIONS

• Knowledge of heavy equipment, its use and maintenance.

• Ability to communicate with management and with men in the field.

• Ability to favorably introduce change in the form of new equipment or new ideas . . . the ability to sell.

EXPERIENCE

• Maintained, shipped, budgeted and set allocation priorities for 85 pieces of heavy equipment as head of a 500-man organization (1975–1977).

MEN AND MACHINERY

• Constructed twelve field operation support complexes, employing a 100-man crew and 19 pieces of heavy equipment (1965–1967).

• Jack-hammer operator, heavy construction (summers 1956–1957–1958).

MANAGEMENT

• Planned, negotiated and executed large-scale equipment purchases on a nation-to-nation level (1972–1974).

SALES

• Achieved field customer acceptance of two major new computer-based systems:

—Equipment inventory control and repair parts expedite system (1968–1971)

—Decision makers' training system (1977–1979)

• Proven leader . . . repeatedly elected or appointed to senior posts.

EDUCATION

B.A. Benedictine College, 1959 (Class President; Yearbook Editor; "Who's Who in American Colleges")

• Naval War College, 1975 (Class President; Graduated "With Highest Distinction")

• University of Maryland, 1973–1974 (Chinese Language)

• Middle Level Management Training Course, 1967–1968 (Class Standing: 1 of 97)

PERSONAL

Family: Sharon and our sons Jim (11), Andy (8) and Matt (5) desire to locate in a Mountain State by 1982; however, in the interim will consider a position elsewhere in or outside the United States . . . Health: Excellent . . . Birthdate: December 9, 1937 . . . Completing Military Service with the rank of Lieutenant Colonel, U.S. Marine Corps.

SUMMARY

A seeker of challenge . . . experienced, proven and confident of closing the sales for profit.

But that simple kind of resume doesn't fare so well, now that we are in the twenty-first century, and post-2008. So, a template would be useful, at this point. A kind of empty form that we could fill in (or fill out) and then post.

I debated putting one here, but sadly I'm afraid I would start to see that template imitated widely, with the thought that this is a form I officially endorse.

And maybe sometimes it wouldn't work. That's a prospect too horrible to contemplate. I would be tarred and feathered, and ridden out of town on a rail. So, I'm not going to give you one, other than the example you already have on page 8.

Fortunately, there are already hundreds of free ones out there. Lots of different ones to choose from. They're on the Internet, of course. Try www.southworth.com; it has a bunch of different templates, submitted by various resume writers.

In addition, www.gotthejob.com/resume_writing_service_samples.html has some interesting samples (in the midst of an attempt to sell you one of their many packages).

Also, www.job-hunt.org/resume-samples/sample-resumes.shtml has some interesting ones, from Susan Ireland.

Beware that there are some sites that advertise "*free* resume templates" but they are our old friends, the "resume-builder" sites, which—as we saw earlier—require registration before they will show you anything, and almost always try to sell you a "package" with a fee attached, halfway in, should you want to print your finished resume or do other follow-up. Among the most common names you will run into, in this broad category, are *Live Career, MyPerfectResume, PongoResume, Resume-now, ResumeGenius, Resumizer,* and *SmartResumeWizard.* Three of these are the same company.

If you read the earlier parts of this guide, you will realize that *many of the resume templates out there violate some of the most basic research I have reported to you in this guide;* viz, they begin with the controversial "Objective," they do not list your key words at the top, they do not sketch out the main outlines of *You* on the top third of the page, they use some of the words that employers say they're sick and tired of, they make empty boasts without evidence, they are absent any numbers or percentages, they do not present You as obsessed with being a profit rather than a cost, and they have no plan for highlighting your "soft skills" (how you get along with people). Most of all, your vitality is missing from the inert page or pages.

All of which is to say, that you are wiser than those templates and examples, and if you pick one, you may need to considerably change, adapt, and edit whichever one you choose, to the point where the final product will likely have only the vaguest resemblance to the template you started with.

You can use the example on page 8 as your initial inspiration. Go from there. Refer to the Q&A that follows. Put your own stamp upon it.

Q&A ABOUT WRITING YOUR RESUME

I know I should put my name and contact information at the top of my resume. How much information should I put there?

You will find various opinions, ranging from *include everything* to *include the least amount possible; not even your home address and maybe not even your phone number. Just your name and your email address.* The reason for this caution is, you guessed it, people out there who are up to no good. You wouldn't leave the door to your home or apartment wide open all night while you slept; don't do that with your resume, either.

Personally, I'd include your name, phone number if someone will always be there to answer (otherwise specify what hours they should call), your email address, and before that your street address and town—to assure them you're a local, and not living out of your car. (Unless you are.)

Should I include a job objective?

Oh, opinions about this range all over the lot. Some employers say emphatically No, others say emphatically Yes.

Personally, I like Alison Doyle's suggestion of a Headline instead of an Objective, right beneath your personal information.* The difference? An Objective describes who you want to be in the future. A Headline describes who you've been up

---

*"How to Write a Resume Headline,"About.com Job Searching,
http://jobsearch.about.com/od/includeinresume/a/resume-headlines.htm.

until now, namely, a person with great experience. A Headline presumes, of course, that you're not looking for a career change. Here are a few of Doyle's headlines, slightly edited:

> Successful Manager of 30 Online Marketing Campaigns
>
> A Chef with Eight Years of Fine Dining Experience
>
> Army Veteran with Determination and Strong Work Ethic
>
> Bilingual Nursing Graduate with Six Years' Experience in Rural Health Care

I know I should put some key words right below my headline or objective. What should I include in those key words?

They should be nouns or phrases, rather than verbs, generally speaking.

If it's your General Resume (the *To Whom It May Concern* type), your key words should include **Fields** that you're familiar with (*such as applied mathematics, fracking, or accounting*), **Special Knowledges** you have (*such as total familiarity with a computerized warehouse management system [WMS], or the Japanese language, or computer programming*), **Skills** you possess (*such as analysis, research, creative imagination*), and any other nouns that an employer would expect to find for the kind of job you're looking for.

If it's a Targeted Resume (the *Dear Mr. or Ms.* type), your key words should take their cue from the employer's job posting that you're responding to. It should repeat every key qualifier in that job posting *that you can legitimately claim of yourself.* And I mean *legitimately.* This is no time for lies, believe me. It might sometimes get you an interview, but then what? You will be discovered as a liar.

Here's an example of how to find key words for a Targeted Resume. I picked this posting at random off the Internet, and I have already capitalized and underlined the key words therein (from the employer's perspective):

> Performance ANALYST working closely with the DHS (Coast Guard) applying human performance technology (HPT) principles. Employee will be conducting PERFORMANCE ASSESSMENTS to monitor workforce readiness and performance.

> Performance analysts will analyze and communicate emergent and long-term WORKFORCE CAPABILITY shortfalls to achieve service-wide standardization.

> EXPERIENCE WORKING WITH HUMAN PERFORMANCE TECHNOLOGY (HPT) PRINCIPLES. PROVEN PERFORMANCE ANALYSIS EXPERIENCE. COAST GUARD EXPERIENCE a plus.

> Must possess a BACHELOR'S DEGREE and 5 YEARS OF RELATED EXPERIENCE OR a MASTER'S DEGREE IN A RELATED FIELD and ONE YEAR OF EXPERIENCE.

Related fields of study include but are not limited to: <u>INSTRUCTIONAL SYSTEMS,</u> <u>INSTRUCTIONAL SYSTEMS TECHNOLOGY,</u> <u>INSTRUCTIONAL & PERFORMANCE TECH-</u> <u>NOLOGY</u> or Education (with <u>A CONCENTRA-</u> <u>TION IN EDUCATIONAL TECHNOLOGY</u>)

A minimum of <u>ONE YEAR EXPERIENCE</u> <u>CONDUCTING PERFORMANCE ANALYSES</u> or <u>FRONT-END ANALYSES.</u>

And <u>PROFICIENT IN USING MICROSOFT</u> <u>WORD, OUTLOOK, EXCEL, POWERPOINT,</u> and <u>COMPUTER GRAPHICS PROGRAMS.</u>

Now what do you have with those words that I have capitalized and underlined above? You have a *potential* list of key words for your resume. I want to stress the word "potential." You must look at each underlined word or phrase and grill yourself: *Do I really have that? Do I REALLY have that?*

If the answer is honestly "Yes," it goes into your key word section at the top of your Targeted Resume. If the answer is a reluctant "No," you DO NOT include it. The rule is, *Never lie.*

And when you're done, you have your key words for your *Targeted Resume* to a particular employer, in response to their job posting.

Don't add anything else to your key word section (why confuse the employer, or send them down a side road?) unless you think it really strengthens your case *for that job!*

What should be the form of the body of my resume, where I list my work history and experience?

In the ancient debate between the chronological form or the functional form, employers today generally prefer the reverse chronological form. The so-called functional form (which focuses on your skills and knowledges minus any dates, rather than on your work history) used to be an equal option, but is now regarded with some suspicion by employers as an attempt to hide either your age or big gaps in your employment history. That doesn't mean you can't use the functional form; it only means you should be aware that it introduces an extra question mark in the minds of many employers.[*]

If I use the chronological form, what do I do about gaps in my work history?

In a chronological resume[**] some experts advise you to put the date range in, for the times when you were employed, don't comment on the gap(s), and just hope some employer will be so intrigued by the rest of your resume that they will call you in anyway, and then you have a chance to explain the gap(s).

Others say that's a gamble, and you should take care that there are no gaps on your resume. For the period(s) when you were out of work, they recommend you put down the dates, and then say "Out of the workforce. Helping raise my

---

[*]For an example, see http://jobsearch.about.com/library/samples/blresumefunct.htm.

[**]For an example, see http://jobsearch.about.com/library/samples/blresumechronolog.htm.

family." Or "Out of the workforce. Studying x, to update my skills, so I could be a stronger asset to my next employer." Or "Out of the workforce. Volunteering at my local x."

I'm a returning vet. I'm not sure how to write a civilian resume.

That's certainly not surprising. Your major problem is going to be one of translation. Our country has lots of subcultures, and each has its own language. When we've been in that subculture and then move out of it, we have to translate our old language into that of the civilian world. For example, clergy live in just such a subculture, and when they move into the civilian world—or as they would say, the secular world—they have to stop talking about their experience as "preaching," for example, and translate that as "teaching."

So it is with your experience in your subculture, the military. Now that you are returning to the civilian world, you have to do some translation. Fortunately, there are a number of websites devoted to helping returning vets, with Military Skills Translators. These include:

> www.careerinfonet.org/moc
> www.onetonline.org/crosswalk
> www.mynextmove.org/vets/find/military
> https://h2h.jobs
> www.dllr.state.md.us/mil2fedjobs

Your second problem will be to pick out a target industry and a target job. Don't just go after *anything*. Then figure out what skills such an industry and job demand, and compare this to the skills you picked up or demonstrated in the military.

There is also www.ClearedJobs.Net, a veteran-owned, security-cleared job board that connects cleared talent with cleared facilities employers.

Lastly, http://WeHireHeroes.com is more popular than three of the top four government-run veteran job sites. So take a look at it, and see if it is of any interest to you. Check out, also, VetJobs.com and HirePatriots.com.

I have a different problem. My age! What can I do about my age? I'm beyond the age of forty (fifty, sixty . . .), but I still need to work, and I want to work.

Well, they're going to find out your age, once they invite you in. Hence, the question here is only about your resume. So, here goes:

Don't list your age or birth date on your resume (**this advice goes for everyone**).

Don't include a photo on your resume (**this advice also goes for everyone**). If you feel your appearance is a definite asset, and you want a photo to be available, put it on your LinkedIn profile. Most employers that you want to find it, will.

If you have a college degree, don't put a date next to it.

List your work history for only the past ten years (**this advice also goes for everyone**). Employers generally feel anything beyond ten years back is ancient history, and totally irrelevant to today's workplace. A man named Fred Trotter put this well, for any age: *"If I knew what I knew four years ago today and that's all I knew today, I'd be out of a job."*

If you have come firmly into the twenty-first century, be sure to list things that prove that (like "I'm on Facebook, LinkedIn, Twitter, Pinterest, and Instagram"). And be sure it's true. Never lie.

Once your resume is complete, concentrate on approaching only organizations that have 250 or fewer employees; they tend to be much less bothered by age than the large monoliths are.

Finally, if you can't find work, don't always assume it's because of your age. And don't assume it's because of your resume. It may be for some other reason entirely (like, employers holding out for *The Perfect Candidate*, who doesn't even exist anywhere in the world except in their mind).

My problem is that I have a handicap. What should I say about that—on my resume?

You will run into a wide variety of opinion about this, if you scan various job advice sites on the Internet.

My own take on it is that you should almost certainly say nothing—on your resume.

You should say everything—if you get an interview. Face to face is the time to discuss this with a prospective employer. Not before.

I want to put a summary of my experience in the top third of my resume, right after the key words. How long should that ideally be?

Experts say it should be a maximum of five to seven sentences, each making a different point.

I would like to include some skills (action verbs) in my ⌐⌐
But I don't know which ones I can legitimately claim. Where
can I find a decent checklist?

An excellent list can be found on JobMob (jobmob.co.il/
blog/positive-resume-action-verbs).*

I don't know if my own self-assessment accurately reflects the
way that others see me. How can I check this out?

There is a wonderful app called Checkster (www.checkster
.com). Scroll down the homepage to click on the button at
the bottom left: *"My Checkster."* You give them the email
addresses of six (or more) of your coworkers, friends, etc.
Checkster will contact them on your behalf, ask them to
evaluate you, then when Checkster gets their answers, it will
strip off their names, so the feedback is now anonymous;
then they'll mash it all together and give you a summary.
It's for your eyes only, unless you want to share it with an
employer for any reason, down the line. And *My Checkster* is
free. A nice gift from its founder, Yves Lermusi.

Where should I put my education on my resume?

The traditional place for it is at the end or toward the end
of your resume. Even if it's one of the four things every
employer looks for, this will carry their eye down to the end
of your resume. Which you want.

Should I say "salary negotiable" near the bottom of my resume?

---

*JobMob is a site maintained by Jacob Share of Israel for job-seekers in his country
and around the world.

No, for three reasons. First of all, that is assumed. Secondly, it shows you are thinking of yourself as a cost, and not as a profit. And lastly, it is one of those phrases employers have seen way too many times already, as we saw earlier. They are tired of it.

Should I include references in my resume?

No, and don't even say "references available upon request." That is assumed. If you land the interview and an employer at that stage wants references, I guarantee you they will ask. And if they ask, at that time, don't ever give someone as a reference without having asked their permission first. Permission is not automatic. Your hoped-for references have the right to decline, and they don't have to give you a reason.

EDIT, EDIT, AND THEN EDIT ONCE MORE

When you're all done writing, *be sure* to have someone (or two someones) read it over and correct every single grammar or spelling mistake before employers ever see it. You must eliminate:

> **An unprofessional email address** (*like: pussycat@ whatever.com*): 76 percent of employers will eliminate you (I mean, *your resume*) if they find these.[*]

> **Typos**: 61 percent of employers will eliminate you if they find these in your resume.[**]

> **Spelling errors**: 43 percent of employers will eliminate you if they find these in your resume.[***]

All of these warnings apply particularly to cover letters.

---

[*]Survey by BeHiring, reported in "Why You Can't Get a Job . . . Recruiting Explained by the Numbers, " Dr. John Sullivan, *ERE,* May 20, 2013, www.ere.net/2013/05/20/ why-you-can't-get-a-job-recruiting-explained-by-the-numbers.

[**]Survey by CareerBuilder, same place.

[***]Survey by Adecco, same place.

DECISION #7: ASCII OR UNIQUE?

Some resume writers become obsessed with electronic resume management ATS systems, and start to think every resume must go through scanning software. As I said earlier, not true. A survey revealed that 60 percent of the Fortune 500 companies surveyed did not electronically scan the resumes they received.

And of those Fortune 500 who do use scanning software, 77 percent said their ATS systems didn't demand special formatting.

So, the normal scary formatting rules you read all over the Internet, about scannable resumes, may actually only apply to 31 percent of the large organizations, and a smaller percentage than that at smaller organizations.

Find that figure unbelievable? Way too low? Okay, then, pluck whatever percentage you want to, out of the air. Just as long as you understand it is by no means 100 percent.

Now, how do you know if a particular company has sophisticated state-of-the-art ATS technology that will scan (and possibly reject) your resume?

You have two routes.

One is, call them and ask them.

The other is, make up two versions of your resume from the get-go.

... the first version as fancy and creative as you want, in its formatting and its look.

Make the second version a plain unembellished scannable copy of it. Then send both versions to each individual targeted organization, from the start. Let them pick and choose which one they prefer.

What are the guidelines for the plain unembellished copy, so that it will get through scanning software? Oh, you can find guidelines in lots of places on the Internet. Just put "How to create a scannable resume" into your search engine. You'll get more answers than you could possibly want. Summarized, they all add up to this:

The resume should be a plain text ASCII formatted document. (Save as plain text—.txt—or Text Only. Rename your document when you save it. Mail it to yourself and print it out to see how it looks. Fix anything that looks off. Then save it again, but not as a PDF file. Scanning software, if it's used, has lots of trouble reading PDFs.) A simple Microsoft Word file will do just nicely.

Don't allow your resume to do what is called "ATS choking": trying to send through the equipment a resume that causes the system to choke. That would include resumes that contain columns, tables, graphics, lines, underlining, italics, logos, borders, headers or footers, or fancy fonts (embellished text such as serif or script fonts). Go for what is called "sans serif." This is a sans serif type font. *This is script*. As for a serif font, this book is printed in it. Easier for a human to read, if you're not a machine.

Other recommendations for formatting?

Margins should be one inch at top and bottom.

Formatted flush left. Font size at least 12 point.

And we are done with the rules for the version of your resume that you want to get safely through scanning software. If that organization has scanning software.

If you're going to mail it (using the good old post office), print it on plain white 28 lb., 8 1/2 × 11 inch paper, printed on only one side, using black ink. (Don't get fancy here; forget about trying to use the colors of the rainbow.)

By the by, your resume *can* be more than one page.

Put it, unstapled, in an 8 1/2 × 11 inch business envelope.

Be sure you put enough postage on it.

On the other hand, if you're going to *email* it, include a plain text version of it in the body of your email, not as an attachment. Employers are very leery of attachments.

Automated filtering software will usually accept resumes that mirror the job posting that the resume is responding to, if it is indeed responding to a job posting.

3 HOW TO CONSTRUCT A WINNING COVER LETTER

ONLY 17 PERCENT

Every resume expert in the world will tell you that you need to send a *cover letter* along with your resume. So, we begin here with a startling fact: according to a recent survey, only 17 percent of employers bother to read a cover letter.[*]

Ouch!

Well, send it anyway.

It's the courteous thing to do.

And it sometimes makes a profound difference in how your resume is received.

---

[*]A survey by BeHiring, reported in "Why You Can't Get a Job . . . Recruiting Explained by the Numbers, " Dr. John Sullivan, *ERE,* May 20, 2013, www.ere.net/2013/05/20/why-you-can't-get-a-job-recruiting-explained-by-the-numbers.

I get this kind of report all the time, from successful job-hunters: *"Cover letter. Make it personal and specific to THAT job. I was directly told in two interviews that my unique cover letter got me in the door. I researched the companies . . ."*

Yes, research the company, keep the cover letter brief, and let it be about *them* more than it is about you.

Here's a bad cover letter to a company that hasn't yet advertised a vacancy (*I didn't make this one up*):

> Hi:
>
> I am looking to be employed in a full-time IT position with your organization. I see myself as a long-term value-added person with an MBA degree from a noted university, and four years' experience maintaining computer systems for a company with 250 employees. Please let me know if you have any openings. My profile can be found on LinkedIn.
>
> > Me

By contrast, here's a good cover letter to the same company (*I did make this one up*):

> Dear Ms. Westfield:
>
> I've been reading about your organization. It has intrigued me greatly. I like that you are trying to help returning veterans, and I'm impressed with your track record in placing over 65 percent of the vets who turn to you for help. That's really remarkable!

I see that you are planning on launching a national campaign next year, with many new materials being written for those in every community who are anxious to help returning vets. If you are hiring for this task, I would love to be considered.

I have enclosed my resume. As it happens, I have had nine years' experience writing just the kind of materials you are planning on creating. I believe that due to my experience I could save you both time and money, over someone new to this kind of task.

Please let me know if you can grant me an interview; I'd be happy to come in at any time convenient to your schedule, to find out more about what you need to make your impending venture a great success.

> Sincerely,
> Meredith Ontwale
> Email: meo@google.com
> Cellphone: 333-444-5555

You may or may not like either or both. There is no such thing as one "right way" to write a cover letter. Tastes vary greatly; what pleases one employer will leave another employer totally unmoved. What feels natural to one job-hunter will feel stilted to another.

But the point is, the first cover letter is all about You; the second is all about Them. And the second one required considerable digging and research about that organization prior to writing that cover letter.

Cover letters can be an essential part of your job-hunt.

Let's consider when a cover letter may be of use to you:

1. When you find an organization you like, it has no known vacancies, but you want to see if they'd like someone with your skills. In which case you send them your General Resume with the second type of cover letter just presented.

2. You see that an organization has a vacancy, and you want to be considered. In which case you send them a Targeted Resume, with a cover letter detailing in short order what your resume will explain at greater length—namely, that you match their job requirements.

   Alternatively, you just send a cover letter without a resume. Many employers these days prefer a cover letter *instead* of your resume. That brief cover letter can summarize all that a longer resume might have covered.

3. You got in for an interview someplace without having to use your resume. Now that you know more fully what the job involves, you want to go home and draft a resume targeted exactly to the job requirements they discussed in the interview,

mailing it to them (email, that is) no later than the next morning, with a cover letter adding anything you forgot to say during the interview, or underlining anything you did say that you now want to particularly emphasize.

Overall, it is wonderful that sending a cover letter is common business practice. In my own thinking, I don't think of it as a "cover letter." I think of it as "Add-A-Note." When your resume is all done, or when an interview is all over, you're back where you live and then suddenly you clap your hand to your head and say, "Oh, *how* could I have forgotten that?" Isn't it wonderful that you can still be rescued? You can always "Add-A-Note." Common business practice!

If you want further guidance in all this, just type "cover letters" into your favorite search engine. You'll be surprised at how many tips, examples, and other information you find. Look especially for Susan Ireland's Cover Letter Guide at http://susanireland.com/letter/how-to. It's good, and it's free.

4 WHERE TO SEND OR POST YOUR RESUME (AND COVER LETTER)

WHERE YOU POST YOUR RESUME MAKES A DIFFERENCE

In this post-2008 economic climate, what is an employer's greatest problem when they advertise that they have a vacancy to fill? You guessed it. Too many resumes. Way too many. Come flooding in.

Employers, large or small, are buried under resumes, these days. The current statistics, as you may recall, are that for each job vacancy or posting that employers put up, they typically receive 250 resumes in response.[*]

It's a real pain for employers, especially small employers, to have to sort through all of those. Half of those 250 haven't got a chance. They are going to be turned down immediately, for one simple reason: they don't come even close to what the employer said were the minimum job requirements. Those

---

[*]Of course, for some vacancies—say, clerk at a local hardware store—the number is much lower. And for other vacancies, such as a software engineer position at a large corporation like Yahoo!, the number is much higher.

job-hunters said to themselves, *This isn't a job I think I have much of a chance at, but I'll put my resume across their path anyway. It can't hurt.*

They are obviously desperate, which is completely understandable in this economy. But in many cases they are also lazy. We know from eye movement studies that on average these days, job-hunters spend only seventy-six seconds reading over the job description before deciding to send in their resume.[*]

I was having lunch last week with a man who hires endlessly for companies experiencing hypergrowth. I asked him what was the chief reason he turned down candidates. He said this one: "They hadn't done any research on that employer, before they came in."

Hopefully you are better than that. But your resume is still buried in there with all those others.

Buried where? Either in their mail, if they are a very small employer (25 or fewer employees). Or on the Internet, if the employer used one of the traditional, familiar Internet sites where employers have traditionally gone to post their openings. (These are called job boards, by the way.)

Once these boards were small: Monster, CareerBuilder, HotJobs, Dice, and the like. Now these places are huge. Monster, for example, allegedly has over one million job

---

*According to a survey of job-hunters' eye movements by TheLadders, reported in "Why You Can't Get a Job . . . Recruiting Explained by the Numbers, " Dr. John Sullivan, *ERE,* May 20, 2013, www.ere.net/2013/05/20/why-you-can't-get-a-job-recruiting-explained-by-the-numbers. Most of those seventy-six seconds is spent looking at just the job title, salary, and location.

postings and over one million resumes, at any one time.*
Monster has 25 million visitors a month; Indeed.com, the
largest job website in the world, has even more: a hundred
million visitors a month.

This compounds employers' problems in finding the right
employee. And it compounds job-hunters' problems in
being found.

It feels to employers like they are looking for a needle in
a haystack.

The bigger the haystack, the harder it is to find the needle.
The smaller the haystack, the easier it is to find the needle.
(*The needle is You.*)

Increasingly, therefore, employers ask themselves, "Where
can I find the smallest haystack? Where would I have to
read or sift through the least number of resumes, before I
decide who to invite in for an interview?"

And here's what they have discovered. This, from an analysis of 1,300,000 job applications and 26,000 hires.**

Job Boards: 219. If employers go looking on an Internet job
board such as CareerBuilder.com or Monster.com, they typically have to look through 219 resumes from job-hunters
who respond to their announcement of a vacancy before
they find someone to hire.

---

*That doesn't therefore mean the site does a good job of matching. As of this writ-
ing, its stock is trading at just $4.24 a share.

**Released in April 2011 by Jobs2web Inc. (now SuccessFactors.com).

Social Media: 116. If employers go looking on social media sites, they typically have to look through 116 resumes before they find someone to hire. Which social media sites, in particular? A survey of one thousand employers found that 93 percent of them searched LinkedIn to find employees, 66 percent searched Facebook, and 54 percent searched Twitter.*

Their Own Website: 33. If employers post their vacancy on their own website, they typically have to look through thirty-three resumes from job-hunters who respond, before they find someone to hire.

Now we come to the strategies where you have to work harder before posting your resume:

Before a Vacancy Is Posted: 32. If job-hunters take the initiative to find out as much as they possibly can about a specific organization or company, and they send their Targeted Resume directly to them—even though that organization doesn't have an advertised vacancy—employers typically have to look through only thirty-two such resumes before they find someone to hire.

Even more work than that, on the job-hunter's part:

An In-House Referral: 10. If the job-hunter takes even more initiative, chooses a company—preferably a smaller company—where they'd like to work, and gets an in-house referral (i.e., gets some employee within that company to recommend them), employers have to look through only ten such resumes before they find someone to hire.

---

*Reported by Jay Moye in his January 3, 2013, article, "Hire Power," at www.coca-colacompany.com/stories/hire-power-how-social-media-is-changing-the-way-people-search-for-jobs.

Now, where do you think knowledgeable employers would prefer to go, to look for a new employee?

The ones that take the least time, of course. The smaller the haystack, the easier it is to find the needle.

So, you'd be wise beyond your years to go where they go: target the smaller haystacks first.

SMALL HAYSTACK #1: THE IN-HOUSE REFERRAL

We'll start with the smallest one, above: the In-House Referral. This involves your choosing which place(s) you want to work for, and then finding someone you know who works there, and is willing to introduce you there and recommend you. And this, whether or not that place has a known vacancy at the time.

The secret to pulling this off used to be something called *networking.* You were encouraged to go to event after event—job fairs, trade shows, college alumni get-togethers, conventions in your field, professional association meetings, chamber of commerce gatherings, volunteer groups in town, visiting famous speakers, visiting local speakers, meetings, religious groups, and job clubs—to collect as many names, contacts, business cards, and email addresses as you possibly could. The idea was that later, down the line, when you needed an in-house referral to a workplace that had attracted your attention, you'd thumb through those cards and hopefully find the right person.

With the arrival of the Internet upon the scene, networking (so you could find a specific in-house referral) became more organized. LinkedIn, in particular, helped tremendously.

ned LinkedIn earlier. It was launched May 5, 2003. It had ,500 members after the first month; it has 277 million members as of this writing, 84 million of them here in the United States. And 40 percent of them check it daily.

In theory, you use LinkedIn to link only to people you already know. This is much abused, in actual practice. Perfect strangers will ask to link to you.

Nonetheless, it is a fertile field for gathering useful names for later in-house referrals. There are all kinds of ways to search, organize, and retrieve information from the site. Plus it has groups you can join for both information sharing and networking purposes. There are over two million such groups on LinkedIn, at this writing, dealing with every subject, field, interest, and kind of job imaginable. You pick and choose. The average user belongs to seven such groups.* Other Internet sites offer groups as well: MeetUp.com, Google+, Pinterest, and Facebook, to name but a few. (Twitter is great for networking, also.)

As of June 2013 all of this was taken to a new level, with the arrival of Chris Russell's ingenious new website, called Jobs with Friends. Instead of starting your job-hunt by choosing companies, then looking for in-house referrals from your networking, it does the opposite: it starts with your friends, treats them as potential in-house referrals, then looks at their companies. The only requirement is that you have a Facebook account and a LinkedIn account.

---

*These stats are from Craig Smith's statistical goldmine, called Digital Marketing Ramblings, found at http://expandedramblings.com, as of October 2013.

It begins (http://friends.careercloud.com) by asking you to let Jobs with Friends have access to the names of your friends on Facebook; it then goes on to ask for the names of your links on LinkedIn. After it has organized all your friends from Facebook and LinkedIn alphabetically, you can search the database in multiple ways. For example, choose "Employed friends" and it will list them, together with where each friend works.

So if you then like one of those places, you can click on a button to find out more about that company. And Jobs with Friends is partners with Indeed.com (mentioned on page 87), so on the same Jobs with Friends page you can ask if there are any job openings there. If not, you can ask for an alert from Indeed when some vacancy does open up there.

Indeed saves you from having to go to thousands of websites, job boards, or company career pages, looking for advertised vacancies (job postings). It does all that for you. And it's free. As is Jobs with Friends.

By itself, Indeed is one of those gigantic haystacks I mentioned. But entered through the portal of Jobs with Friends, it is a much smaller haystack.

If Indeed turns up a vacancy at an organization you see, and like, on your Jobs with Friends page, you don't have to go networking in search of an in-house referral. You already have that, and Jobs with Friends will help you write a letter asking them to refer and recommend you. Moreover, there is a provision for you to send that friend your resume—preferably one targeted to the specific requirements of that vacancy there.

And of course you can contact the company through your friend even if there is no known vacancy at that time.

The only catch to all this is that, in the time-honored tradition of new and growing websites, your friends/in-house referrals must first join Jobs with Friends themselves.

It's a relatively new site, but it looks promising, and as it matures, it has the potential to help you a lot with introducing your resume into the smallest haystack there is.

SMALL HAYSTACK #2: AN EMPLOYER'S WEBSITE

This involves posting your resume right on the actual websites of companies that interest you, if they have a site, and if their site permits that. This, of course, assumes you have first figured out the place(s) where you would most like to work.

In this post-2008 period, I recommend you pay particular attention to small employers (25 or fewer employees, 50 or fewer, 100 or fewer), and to newer organizations (7 years old or less).

SMALL HAYSTACK #3: NICHE JOB SITES

As we saw earlier, job boards can be huge. But there are small job boards too. And you usually have a much better chance there. Smaller haystack, bigger needle.

These are called "niche sites." They target particular niches. There seems to be a small niche site for just about everything you can think of. Some cover just certain geographical areas—state, region, city or local area—and/or just one industry or profession or field.

Sixty-two percent of all open jobs are posted to niche job sites.

Randall and Katherine Hansen have a nice list of them at www.quintcareers.com/indres.html.

Here are some sample niche sites just so you'll get an idea of their range. If any of these interest you, you can look up their exact URL by putting their name (highlighted in bold, here) into a search engine like Google; though in most cases, just adding ".com" to the names here will take you right to the site in question:

> **AbsolutelyHealthCare**, aka **HealthJobsUSA**: for health care and medical jobs.
>
> **Adrants**: for advertising jobs.
>
> **AllHealthcareJobs**: for health care professionals.
>
> **AllRetailJobs**: for the retail industry (their #1 job board).
>
> **AuthenticJobs**: for web designers and developers seeking freelance opportunities or full-time jobs.
>
> **ClearanceJobs**: for candidates with U.S. government security clearances.
>
> **CollegeRecruiter**: for college students looking for internships or entry-level jobs.
>
> **Coroflot**: for the arts and design positions.
>
> **CrunchBoard**: for Internet and tech jobs.
>
> **Dice**: for tech jobs (one of the largest niche sites, but still niche).

DiversityJobs: for multilingual and multicultural professionals, Hispanics in particular.

eFinancialCareers: for professionals working in the banking and finance industry.

Energyfolks: for energy professionals and students seeking internships or jobs.

FinancialJobBank: for professionals in the accounting and finance industry.

FlexJobs: for full-time or part-time jobs involving flextime or telecommuting.

GitHubJobs: for programmers and developers.

Headhunter: for professional management and executive jobs.

HealthcareJobsite: for jobs in the health care industry.

Hourly: for jobs that are, well, you can guess this one, I'm sure.

iCrunchData: for jobs in business intelligence, big data, cloud, mobile, software and analytics, statistics, technology.

Internmatch: for internships.

IT Job Pro: for jobs in information technology.

Joblux: for jobs in luxury industries, fashion, beauty, design, jewelry.

JobsInLogistics: for jobs in the logistics industry.

JobsInManufacturing: for jobs in engineering, logistics, maintenance, materials management, plant management, and purchasing.

JobsInMotion: for transportation and logistics jobs.

JobsInTrucks: for drivers.

Krop: for creative and tech jobs.

Laimoon: for jobs in Qatar and the UAE.

Levo League: for young professionals seeking meaningful jobs.

Mediabistro: for all kinds of jobs in all kinds of media.

MedReps: for medical sales people.

Miracle Workers: for jobs in health care.

MoneyJobs: for finance or accounting jobs.

paidContent: for digital media content professionals of all kinds.

Sales Gravy: for jobs in sales of all kinds.

Shiftgig: for restaurant and bartending jobs.

SnagAJob: for hourly jobs.

Sologig: for jobs in information technology and engineering.

StackOverflowCareers: for programming and engineering jobs.

TalentZoo: for advertising, marketing, design, and creative jobs as well as jobs for geeks (their nomenclature).

Tech Careers: for IT and tech jobs.

Teens in Tech Labs: for young entrepreneurs worldwide.

WorkInRetail: for bartending jobs, cooks and waiters, restaurant managers, cashiers, store managers, and apparel, jewelry, and merchandise jobs.

PLAN B: WHEN THIS SEEMS LIKE TOO MUCH TROUBLE

If trying to target these smaller haystacks feels like just too much trouble, there are resume distribution services that, for a fee of around fifty bucks, will put your resume up on fifty to ninety of the larger haystacks—the job boards like Monster, CareerBuilder, and Dice. Such distribution firms have names like Resume Boomer, Resume Director, Resume Rabbit (see www.forwardyourresume.com for very useful evaluations of the top ten such services). Whether it will pay you to use one of these services or not is, in my opinion, largely a matter of luck. Blind, dumb luck. I wouldn't do it, but maybe you have the fifty bucks to spend. (Or to waste? Hard to tell.) There are already between 78,900,000 to 200,000,000 resumes and curricula vitae (CVs) floating out there in digital space. Just sayin'. Big, big haystack!!

BYPASSING TRADITIONAL JOB BOARDS

Craigslist has turned out to be a terrific place for job-hunters to post their resume. It's not a job site per se, but it is hugely popular. Sometimes the most popular place is where intersections occur, and intersections are often the key to stumbling across pure, dumb luck.

IN CONCLUSION

There are other ways to find work than just using resumes. But resumes are here to stay, and our job is to make them the best that we can, so that they are the most effective they can be. In the service of this task, research, long overdue, is starting to come in. We know a lot more now about what makes resumes work, and what makes them not work, than we did even ten years ago. We do know how to make them better. In this guide, I have described the research in detail. Or rather, the findings from that research.

And what is the sum of all those findings? It seems contradictory, but it turns out that the more we take the focus off ourselves, and the more we put it on The Other, the easier it is to find a job.

It reminds me of the old saying, that there are two kinds of people who may come into a room where you are sitting by yourself. The first runs in and announces, in a self-absorbed manner, "Well, here I am."

The second comes into the room and their face lights up, as they say, "Ah, there You are."

If your resume shouts out, "Here I am," it will not work as well as it should. But if it says to an employer, "Ah, there You are," doors will open, and you may glimpse a garden just beyond.

ABOUT THE AUTHOR

Dick Bolles—more formally known as Richard Nelson Bolles—is the author of *What Color Is Your Parachute? A Practical Guide for Job-Hunters and Career-Changers*, the most popular job-hunting book in the world. The book has sold more than ten million copies to date, and is dramatically updated, reshaped, and rewritten, every year, in English. "Parachute," as it's often called, has been translated into twenty languages and is used in twenty-six countries. Dick is credited with founding the modern career counseling field, and is often described as the field's #1 celebrity.

What Color Is Your Parachute? was chosen as one of the 100 All-TIME best and most influential nonfiction books published since 1923, by *Time* magazine.

It was chosen as one of twenty-five books that have shaped people's lives (down through history) by the Library of Congress's Center for the Book.

It was chosen as one of the books since 1758 that have helped shape the world of work, by the U.S. Department of Labor.

Dick Bolles was chosen by *Forbes* magazine as one of the "Wealth Wizards" in the United States (along with Warren Buffett and eighteen others), for all the jobs he has helped create.

He is the recipient of the National Samaritan Award (previous honorees include Karl Menninger, Betty Ford, and Peter Drucker).

He has his own websites: www.jobhuntersbible.com and www.eParachute.com. He has a public Facebook page: www.facebook.com/dick.bolles.1.

He is also one of LinkedIn's 500+ "Influencers" and writes regularly for that platform, as well as for Google+ and a number of others.

He is the father of four grown children: Stephen, Sharon, Gary, and Mark (deceased). He also raised a stepdaughter, Serena, in a former marriage. He and his wife, Marci, live in the San Francisco Bay Area.

INDEX

Photos, 27, 73
Picasa, 25
Pinterest, 26, 90
Plaxo, 26
Pontow, Regina, 14
Privacy settings, 22
Procrastination, 63
Professional resume writers,
33–37
Profiles, online, 26–28
Profit, focusing on, 48–53
Publications, 62

R

References, 76
Referrals, in-house, 88–92
Rejections
    Google searches and,
    23–24
    reasons for, 86
Reppler.com, 25
Research
    on employers, 86
    importance of, 86
Responsibilities, 58–59
Resume distribution
    services, 96
Resumes
    average attention paid to,
    by employers, 5–6, 12
    chronological vs.
    functional, 71
    contact information on,
    67, 76
    cover letter sent instead
    of, 83
    dates on, 47, 54, 71–72, 73
    editing, 76
    education on, 54–55, 75
    as elimination game, 12–13,
    15–17, 32
    emailing, 79
    empty claims on, 44–47
    examples of, 8–11, 64
    experience summary
    on, 74
    focus of effective, 97
    formatting, 77–79
    general vs. targeted, 41–44
    headline on, 67–68
    job objective on, 67–68
    key words on, 6–7, 68–70
    leaving out anything
    disturbing, 20
    length of, 7, 79
    lying on, 24, 40
    mailing, 79
    numbers on, 47–48, 51
    painting metaphor for,
    3–7, 31
    photo on, 73
    posting, 85–96
    purpose of, 34–35
    references and, 76
    scanning of, 13–15, 32, 77–79
    soft skills and, 20
    per vacancy, 12, 85–89
    work history on, 54,
    71–72, 73
    yesterday's vs. today's, 2
    See also Google "resume"

ADDITIONAL HELPFUL RESOURCES FROM THE AUTHOR

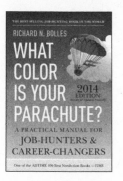

What Color is Your Parachute? 2014

The best-selling job-hunting book in the world by Richard N. Bolles

Trade Paperback ISBN: 9781607743620
eBook ISBN: 9781607743644

The Job-Hunter's Survival Guide

A quick guide for when time is of the essence by Richard N. Bolles

Trade Paperback ISBN: 9781580080262
eBook ISBN: 9780307759429

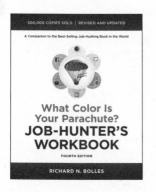

**What Color Is Your Parachute?
Job-Hunter's Workbook,
Fourth Edition**

A fill-in edition of the famous Flower Exercise by Richard N. Bolles

Trade Paperback ISBN: 9781607744979

**What Color Is Your Parachute?
Job-Hunter's Workbook,
Tablet Edition**

An interactive edition for your iPad and Nook by Richard N. Bolles

iPad ISBN: 9781607745792
Nook ISBN: 9781607746041

Visit JobHuntersBible.com and eParachute.com

What Color Is Your Parachute? for Teens, Second Edition

Richard N. Bolles presents advice tailored for high schoolers by Carol Christen, a *Parachute* expert and teenage specialist

Trade Paperback ISBN: 9781580081412
eBook ISBN: 9781607743309

What Color Is Your Parachute? for Retirement, Second Edition

Richard N. Bolles presents retirement advice from John E. Nelson, *Parachute* expert and aging specialist

Trade Paperback ISBN: 9781580082051
eBook ISBN: 9781607743316

The Career Counselor's Handbook, Second Edition

A complete guide for practicing or aspiring career counselors by Howard Figler and Richard N. Bolles

Trade Paperback ISBN: 9781580088701
eBook ISBN: 9781607743552

What Color Is Your Parachute? Guide to Job-Hunting Online, Sixth Edition

Internet job-search tips from Mark Emery Bolles and Richard N. Bolles

Trade Paperback ISBN: 9781607740339
eBook ISBN: 9781607740421

Available from TEN SPEED PRESS wherever books are sold.

www.tenspeed.com